RECORDED VERSIONS
GUITAR
AUTHENTIC TRANSCRIPTIONS
WITH NOTES AND TABLATURE

MW01097727

BULLET FOR MY VALENTINE
FEVER

ISBN 978-1-4234-9676-2

HAL•LEONARD®
CORPORATION

7777 W. BLUEMOUND RD. P.O. BOX 13819 MILWAUKEE, WI 53213

Visit Hal Leonard Online at
www.halleonard.com

Arranged by Olly Weeks
Edited by Alex Davis & Lucy Holliday

Original design and Photography by P.R.Brown

Printed in England by Caligraving Ltd

BULLET FOR MY VALENTINE
FEVER

YOUR BETRAYAL

Words and Music by Matthew Tuck, Jason James,
Michael Thomas and Michael Paget

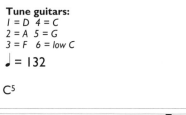

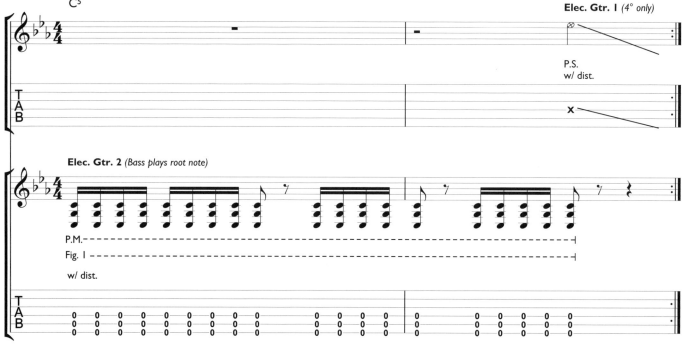

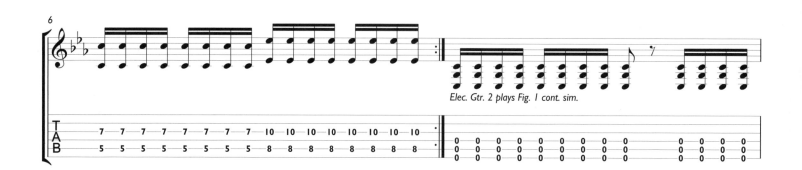

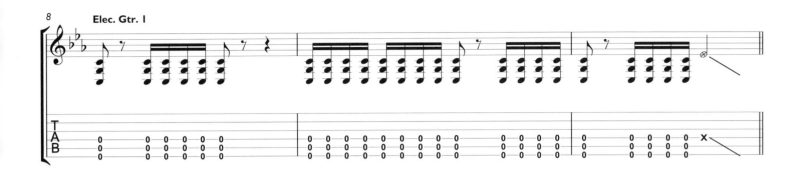

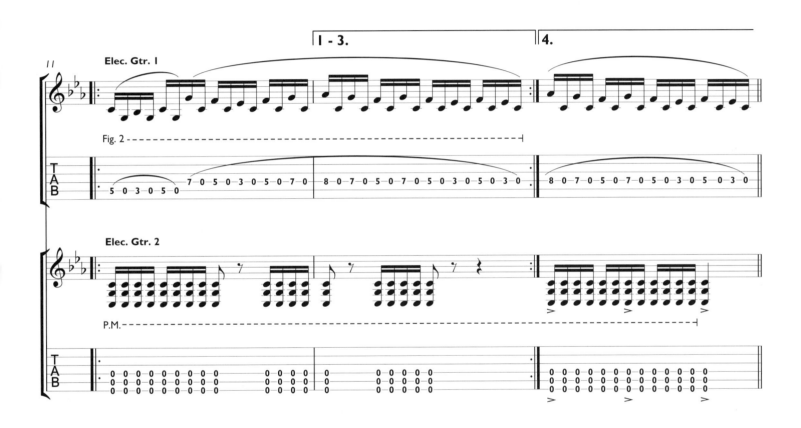

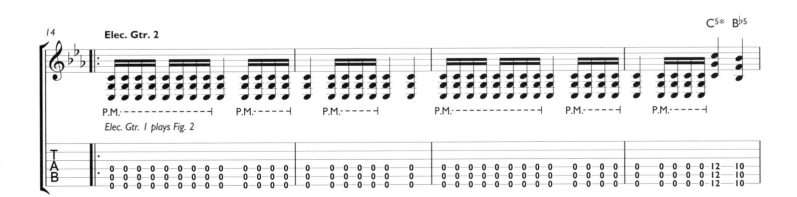

8

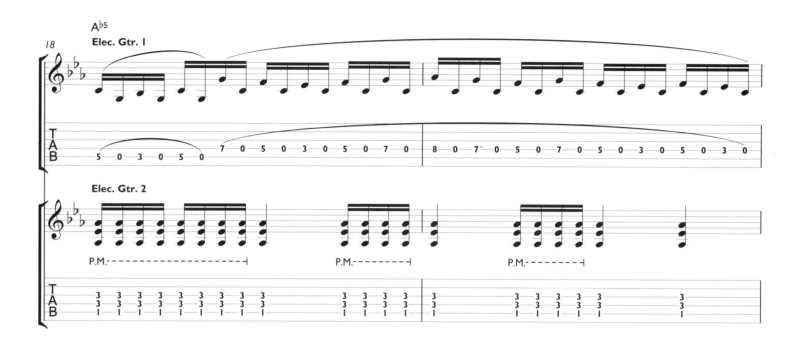

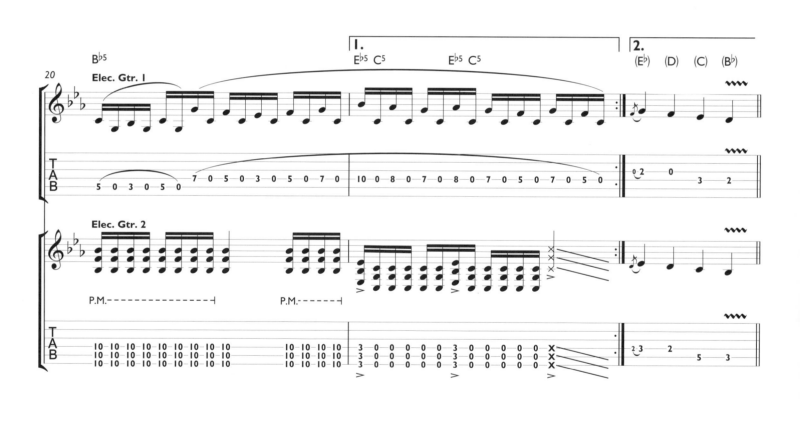

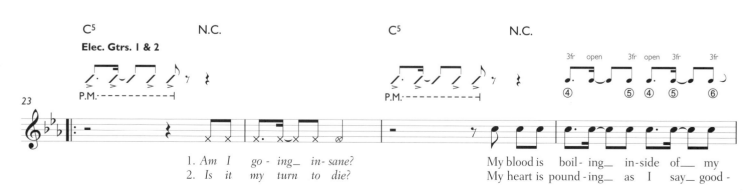

1. Am I go - ing_ in - sane?
2. Is it my turn to die?

My blood is boil - ing_ in - side of_ my
My heart is pound - ing_ as I say_ good -

- brace.)
- brace.)

So here we are,   I'm in your___ head,___   *I'm in___ your heart.*

You   were told   to   run a - way,___   soak   the place   and   light the flame,-

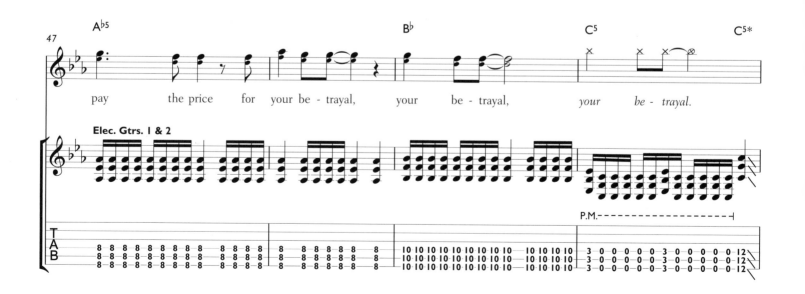

pay   the price   for your be - trayal,   your   be - trayal,   *your   be - trayal.*

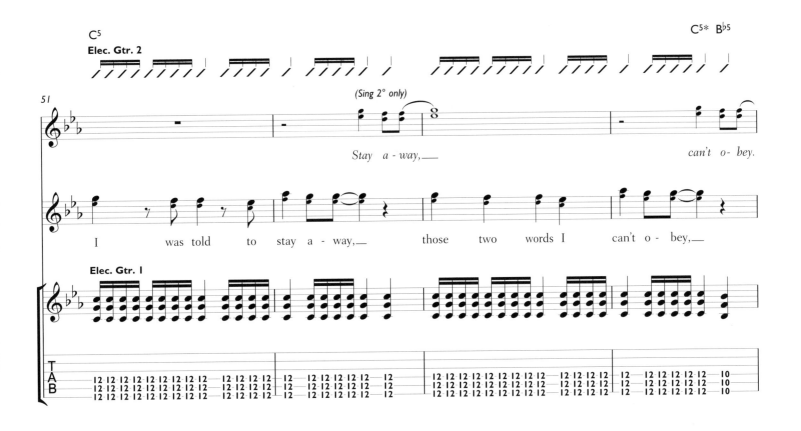

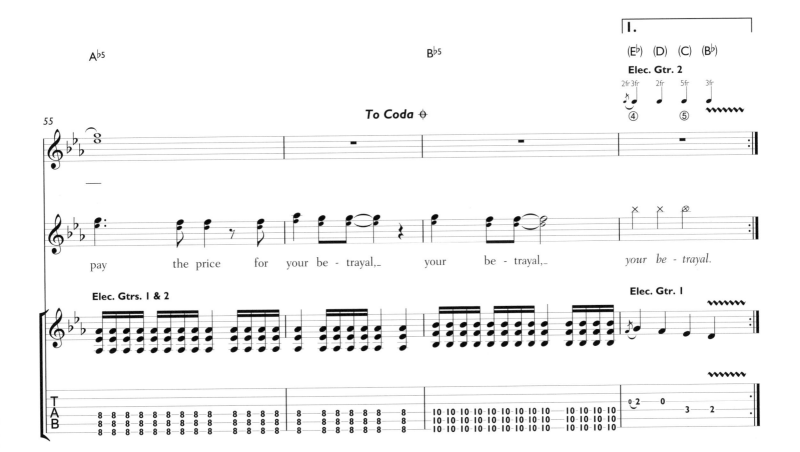

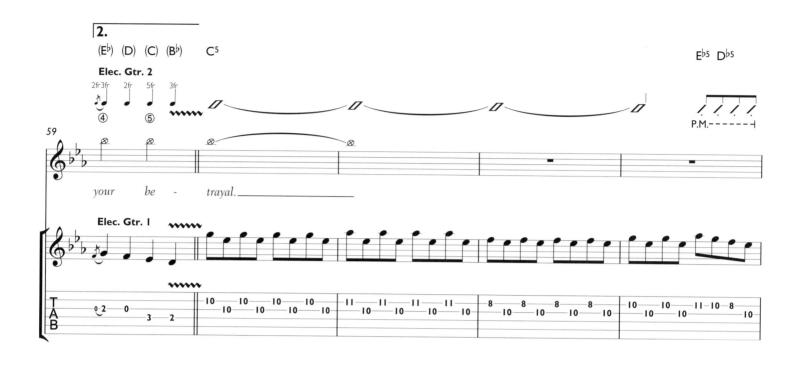

your be - trayal.

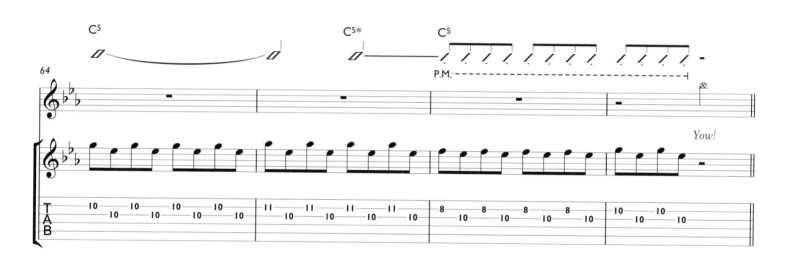

Yow!

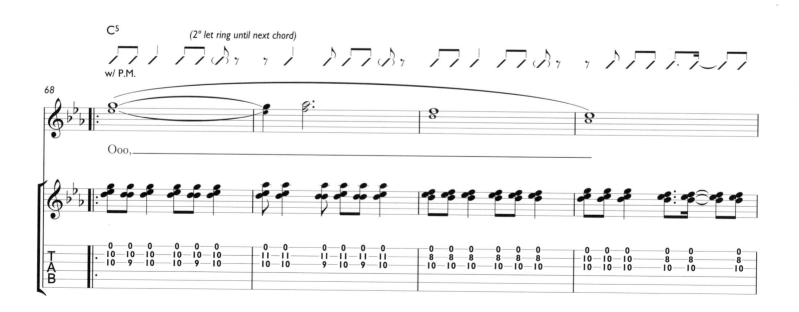

Ooo,

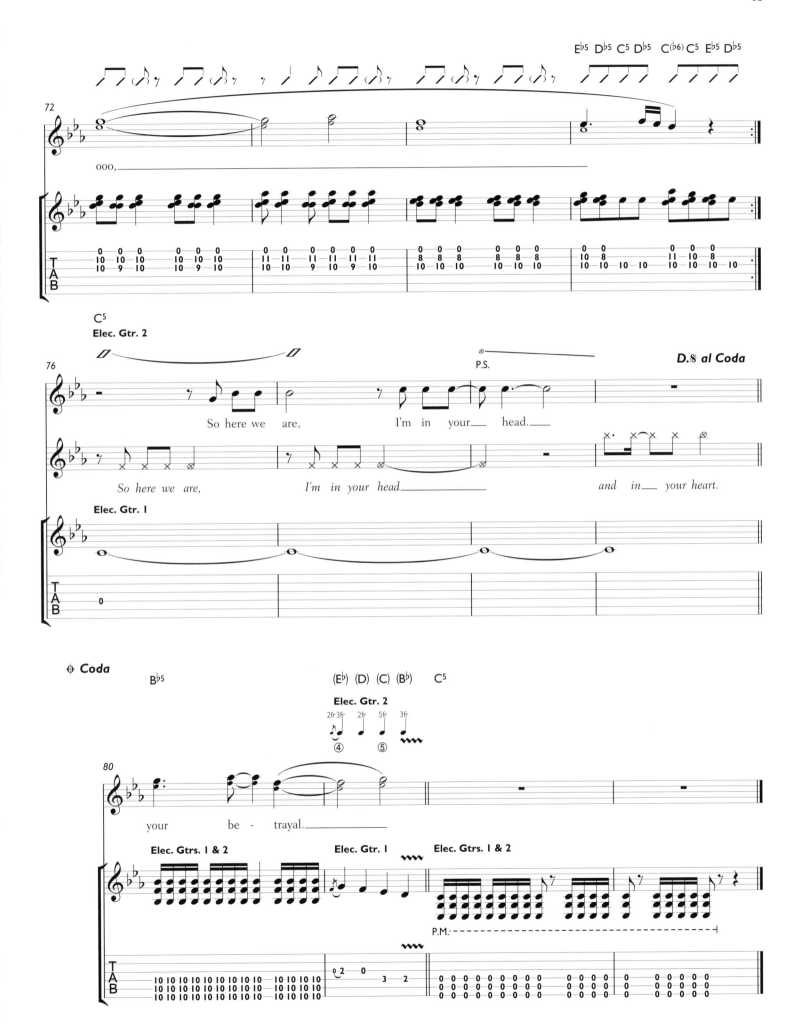

FEVER

Words and Music by Matthew Tuck, Jason James,
Michael Thomas and Michael Paget

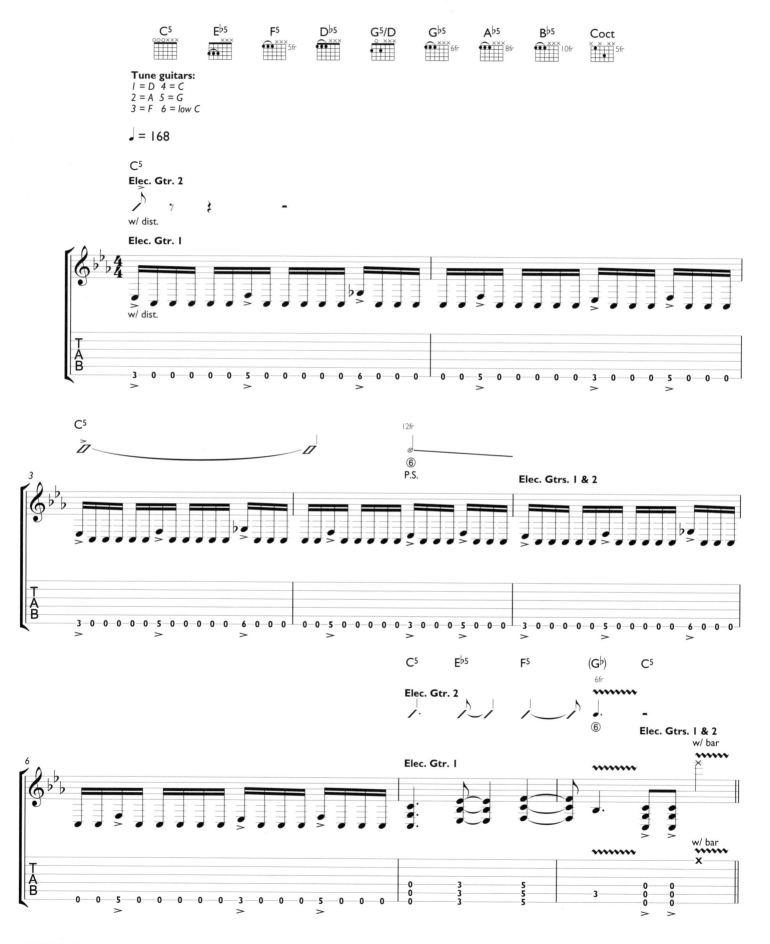

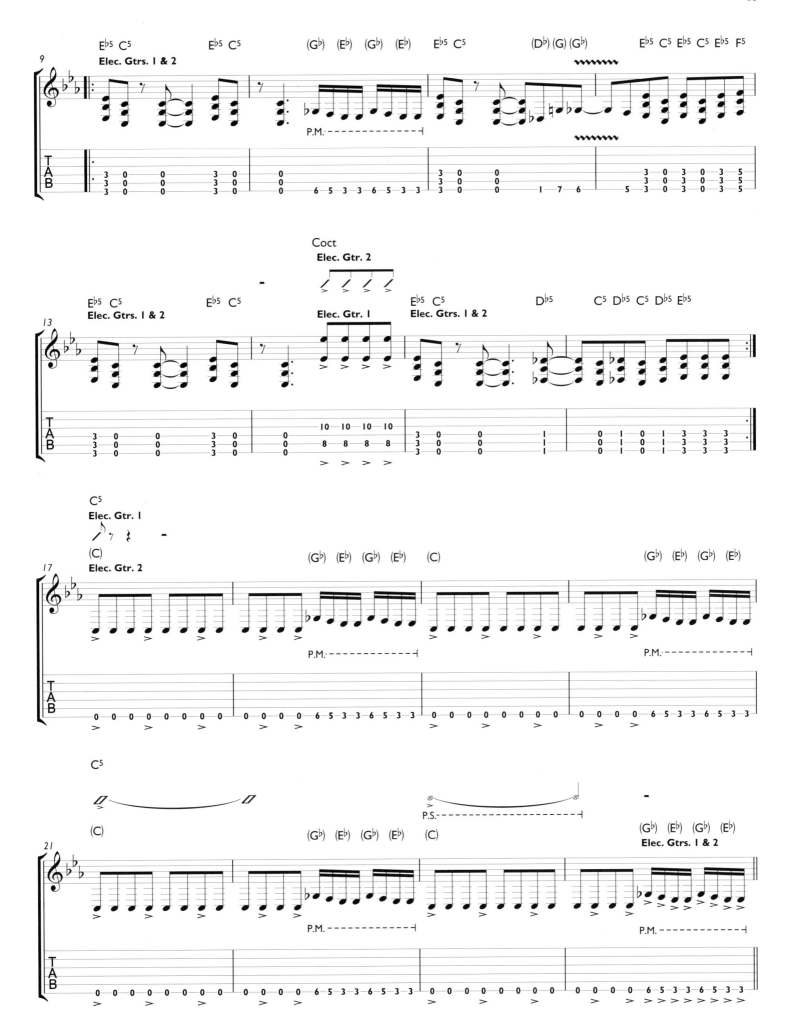

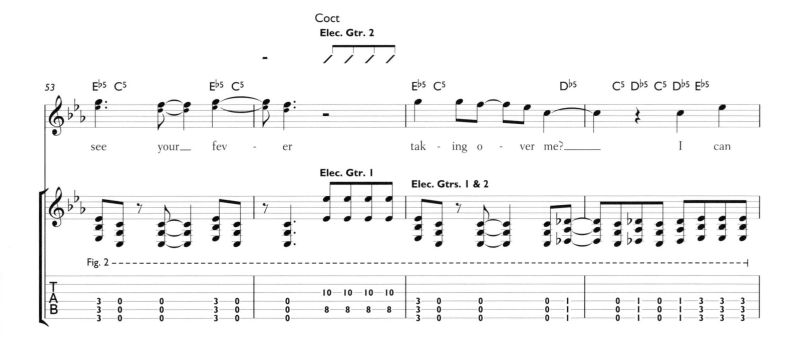

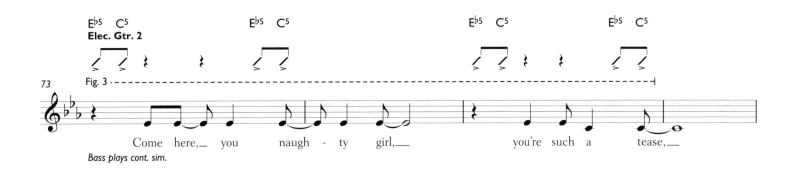

Come here,— you naugh - ty girl,— you're such a tease,—

you look so beau - ti - ful— down on your knees,—

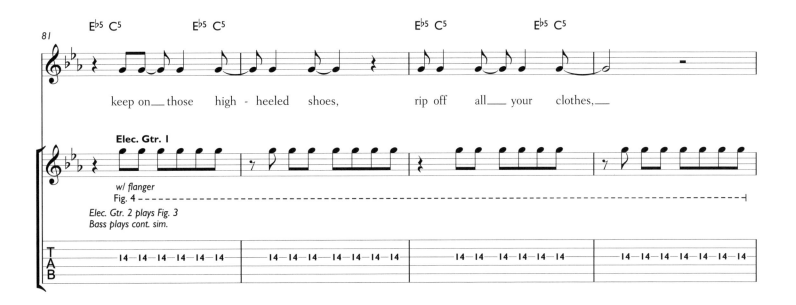

keep on— those high - heeled shoes, rip off all— your clothes,—

you smell so fuck-ing good, you make me lose— con - trol.—

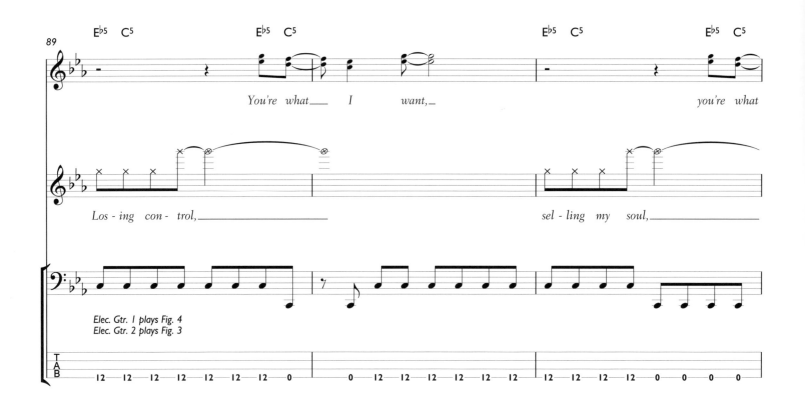

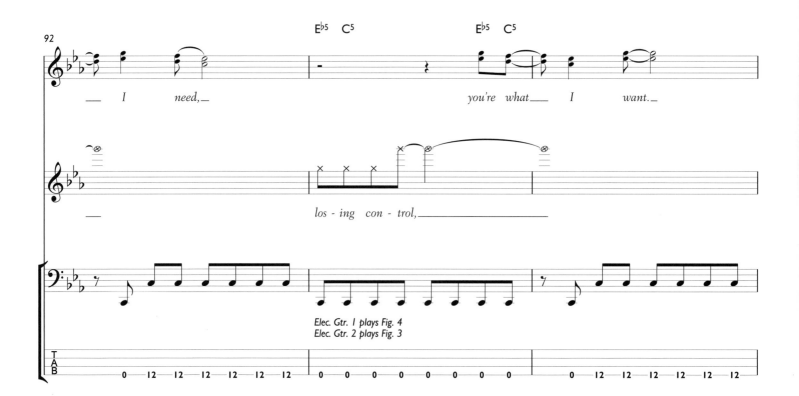

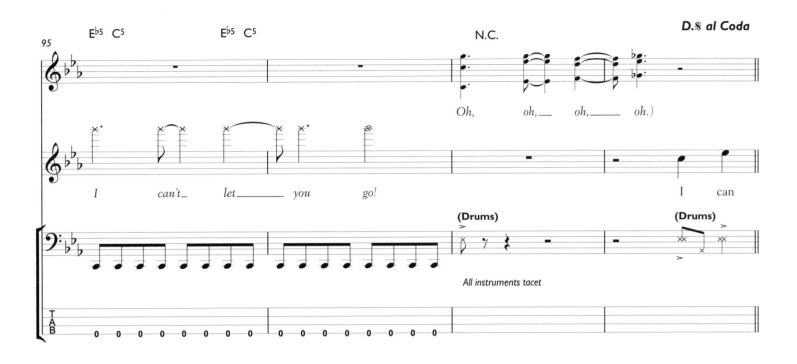

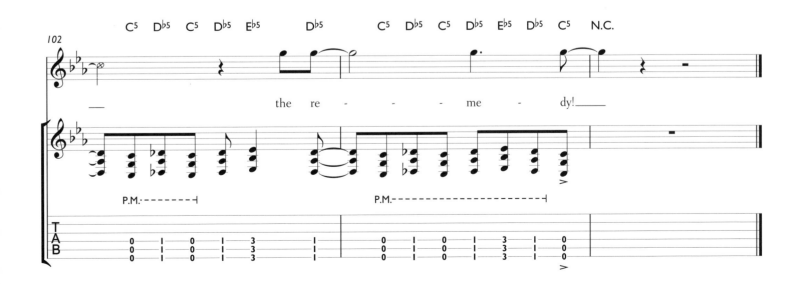

THE LAST FIGHT

Words and Music by Matthew Tuck, Jason James,
Michael Thomas and Michael Paget

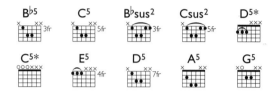

Tune guitars:
1 = D 4 = C
2 = A 5 = G
3 = F 6 = low C

♩ = 168

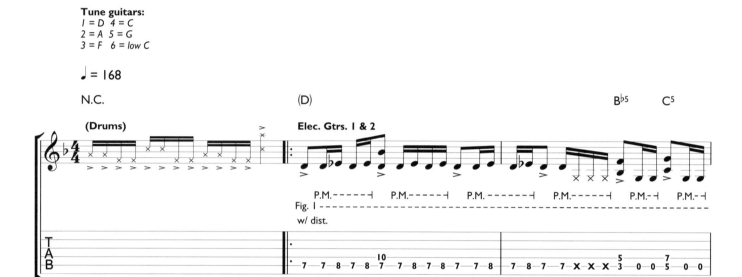

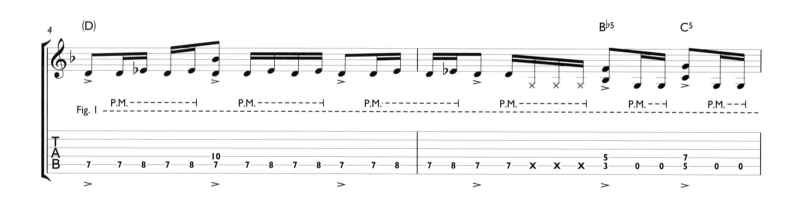

Page 23.

Images.

Lyrics.

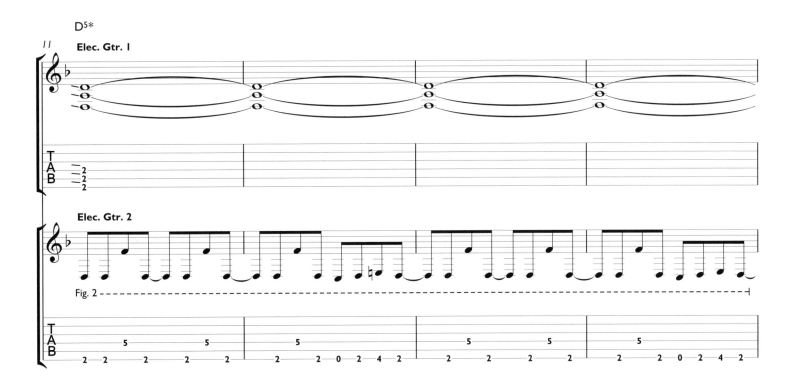

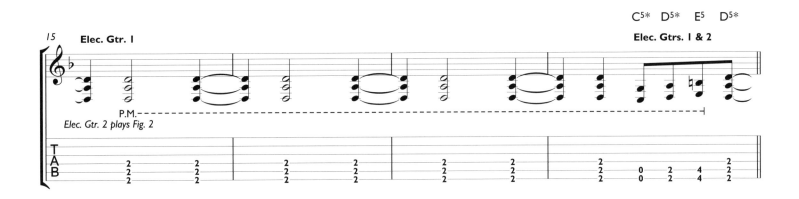

1. I don't wan-na stand__ be-side__ you, I don't wan-na try__ and feel__ the pain
2. Ev'ry-one is sick__ of car-ing, no__ sil-ver lin-ing on__ the cloud

do I fight___ or let___ it die?___

I will

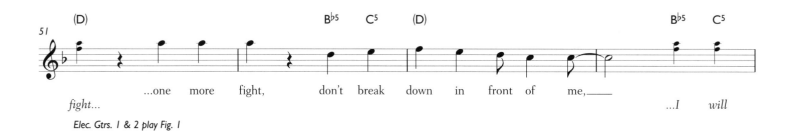

...one more fight, don't break down in front of me,___

...I will

fight...

Elec. Gtrs. 1 & 2 play Fig. 1

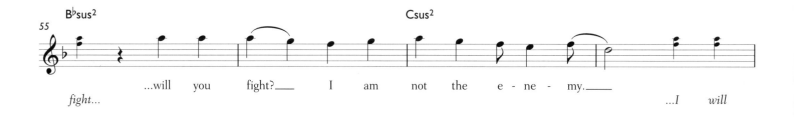

...will you fight?___ I am not the e - ne - my.___

...I will

fight...

...one last time, are you e - ven lis - ten - ing?___

...I will

try...

...the last fight,___ I am not your

fight...

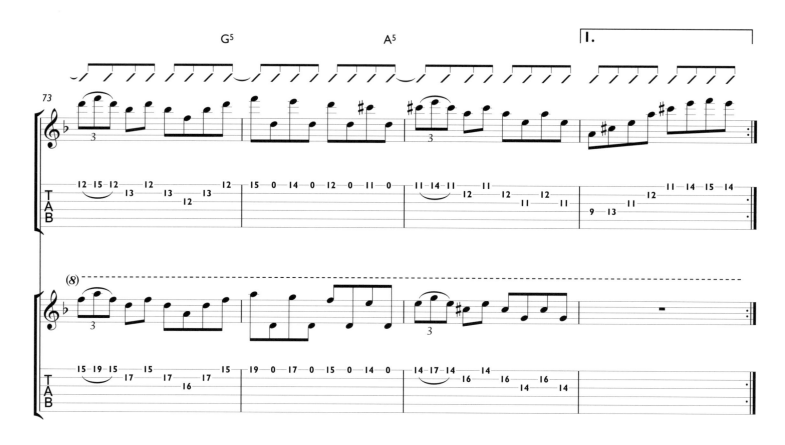

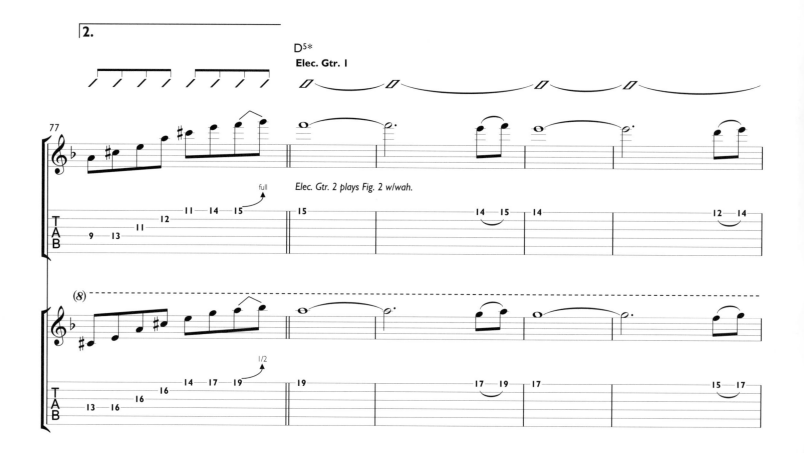

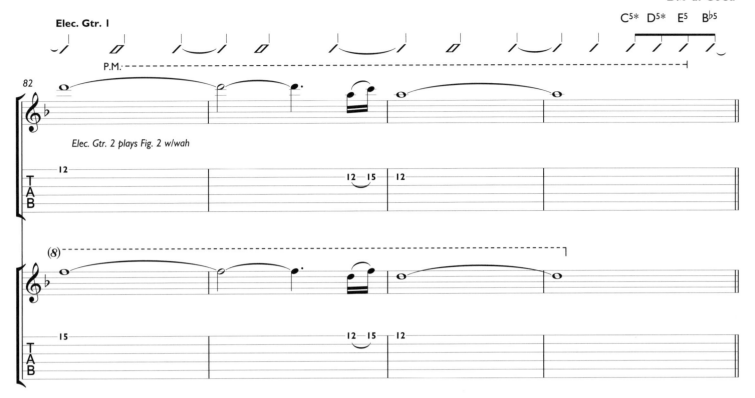

♦ Coda

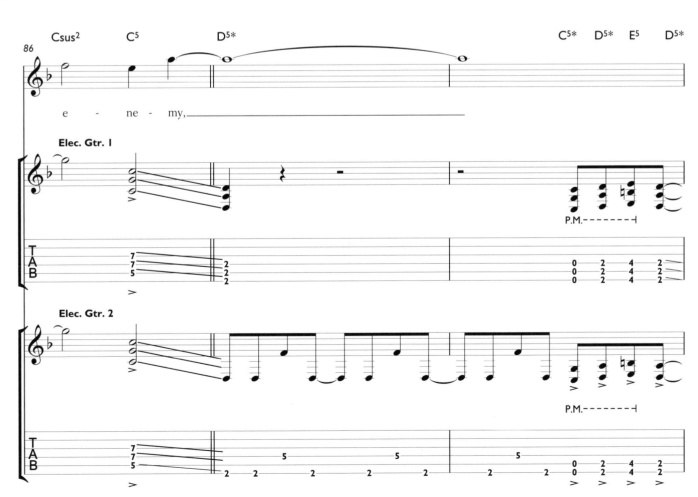

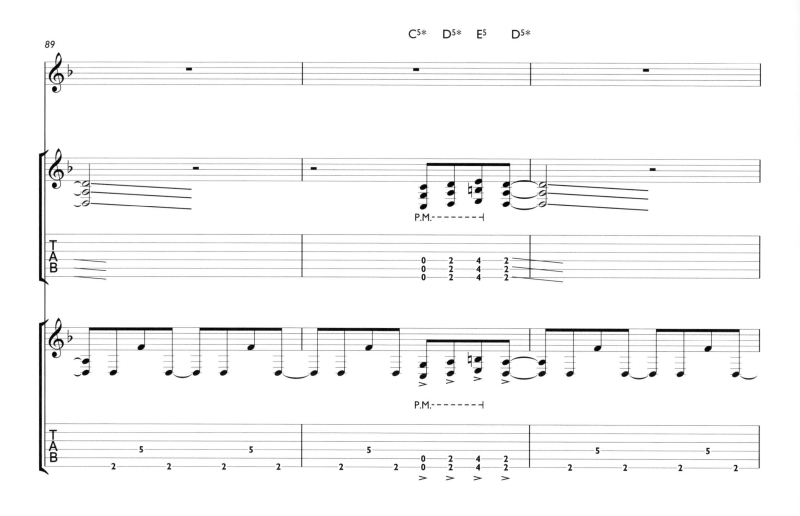

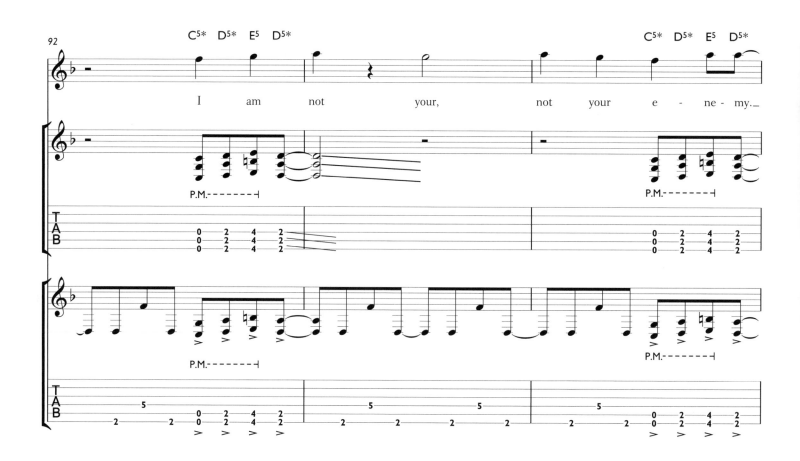

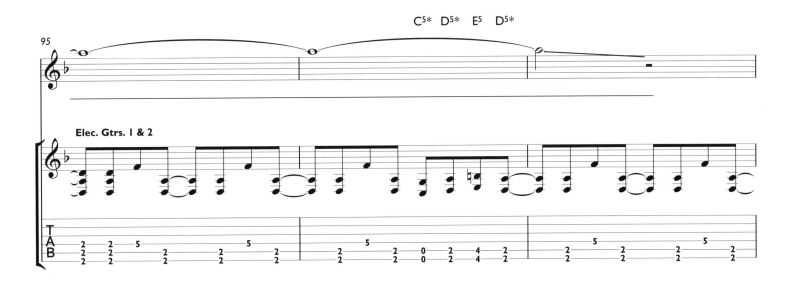

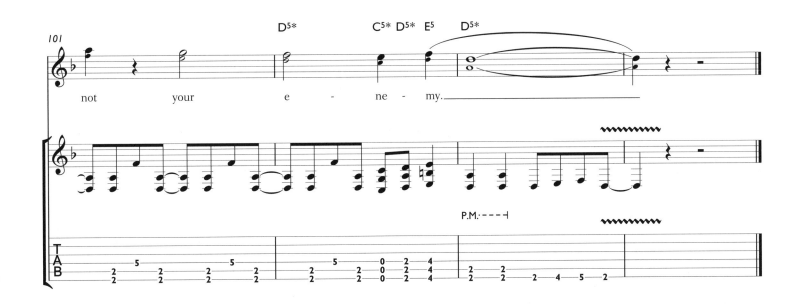

A PLACE WHERE YOU BELONG

Words and Music by Matthew Tuck, Jason James,
Michael Thomas and Michael Paget

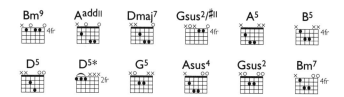

Tune guitars:
1 = D 4 = C
2 = A 5 = G
3 = F 6 = low C

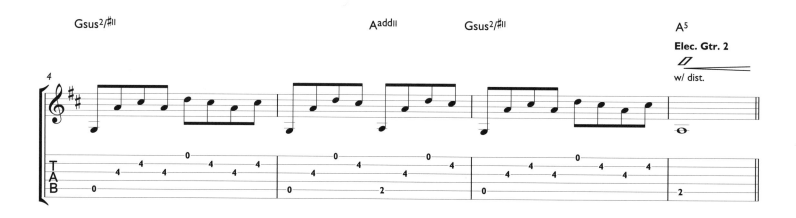

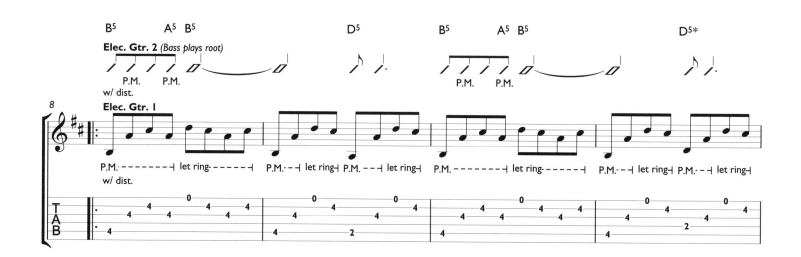

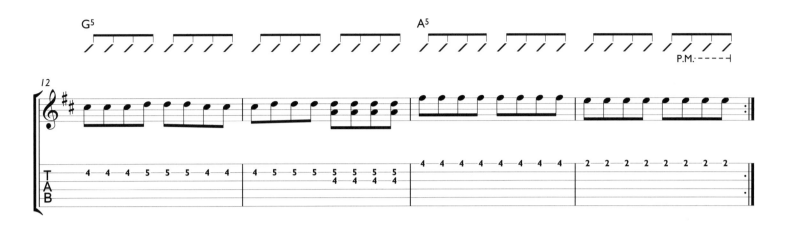

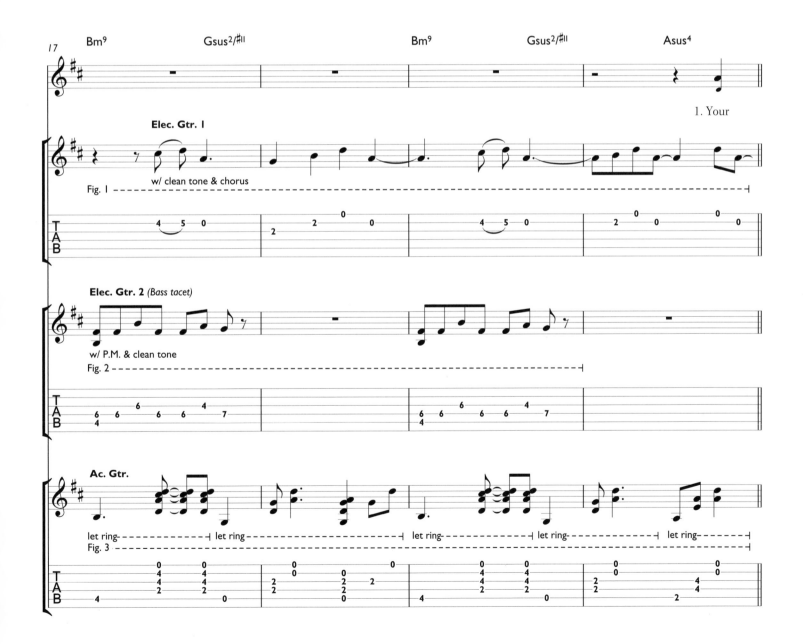

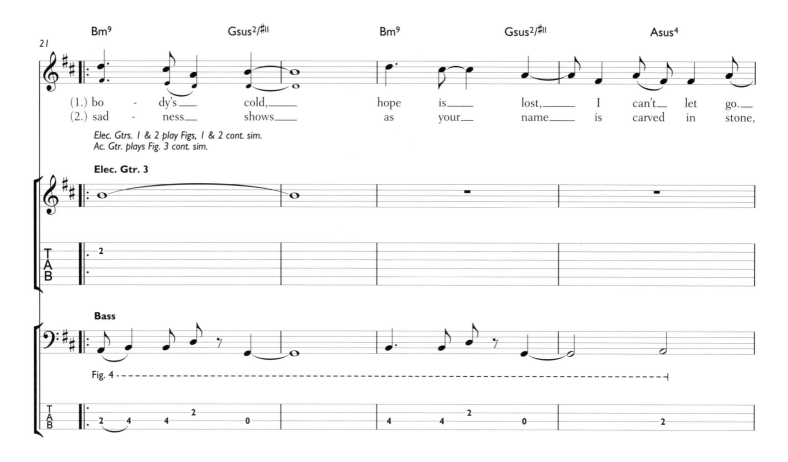

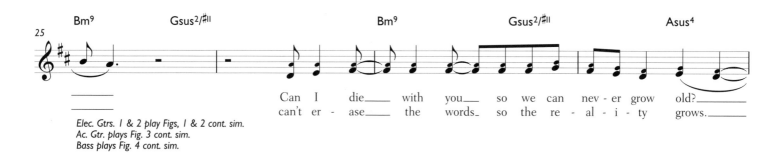

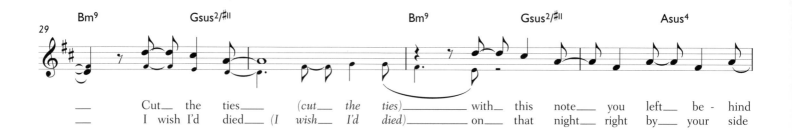

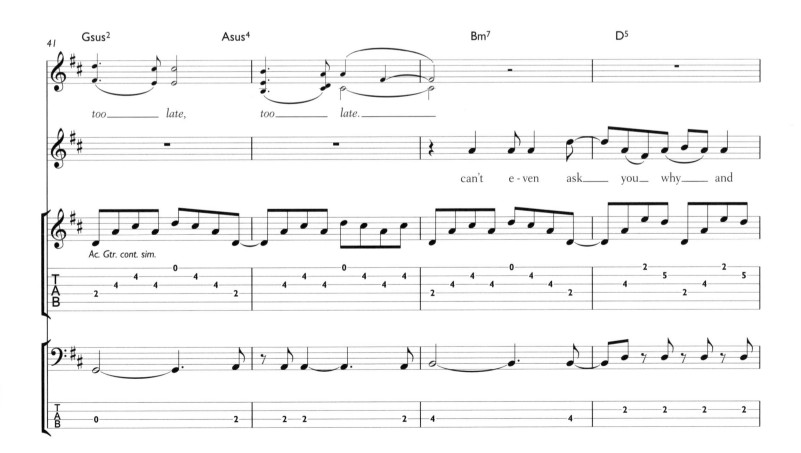

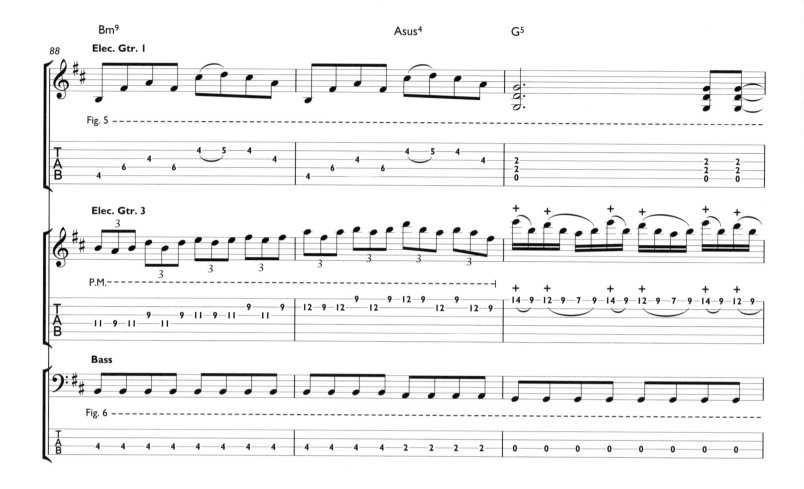

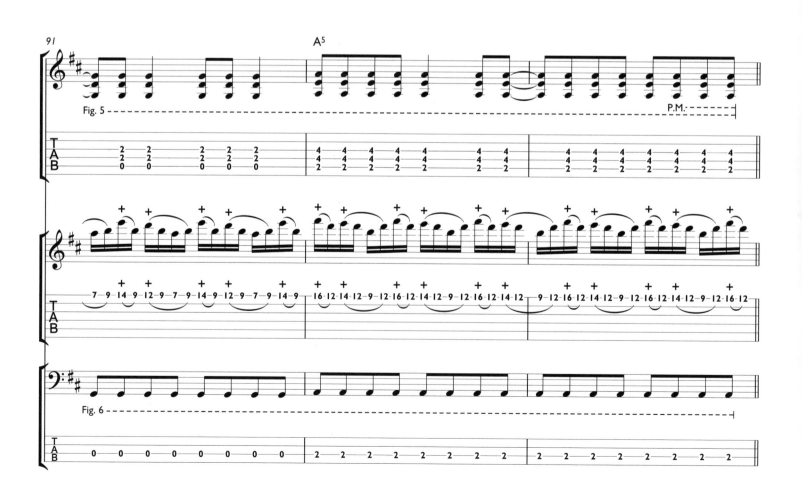

42

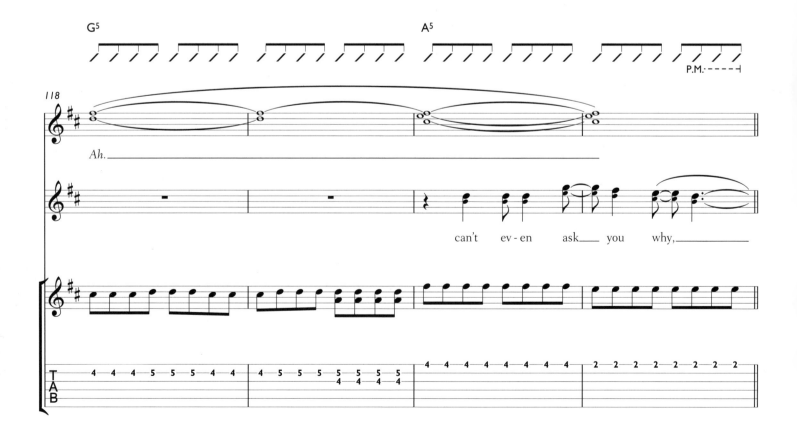

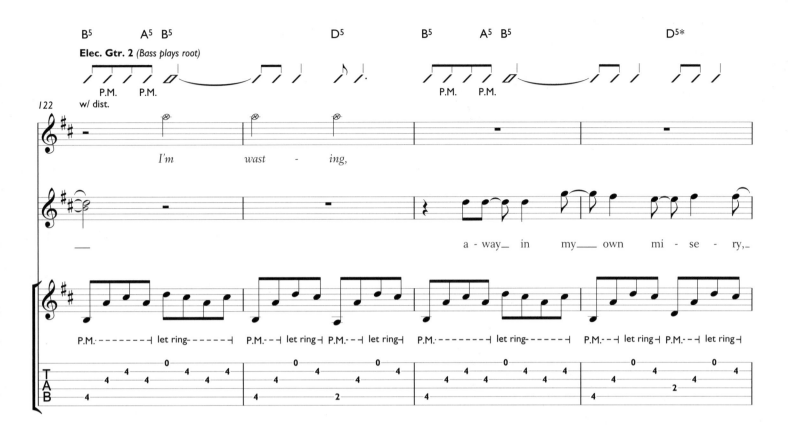

PLEASURE AND PAIN

Words and Music by Matthew Tuck, Jason James,
Michael Thomas and Michael Paget

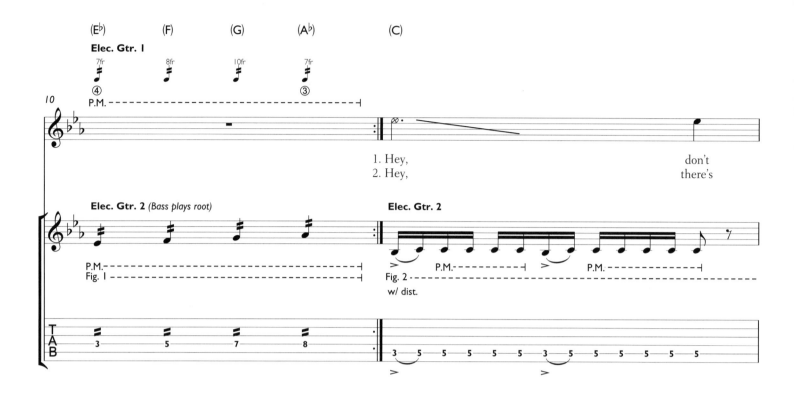

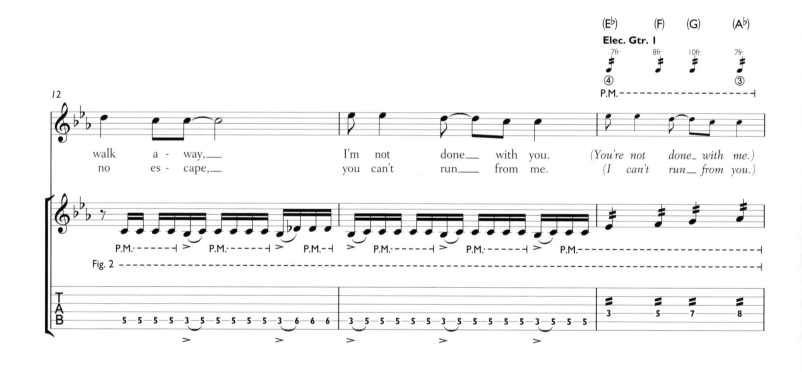

48

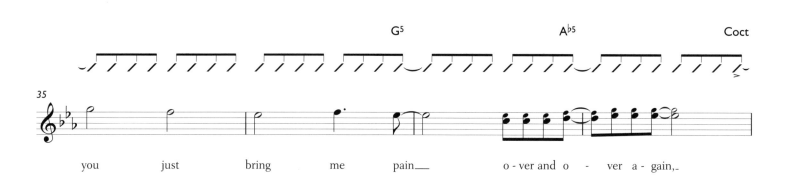

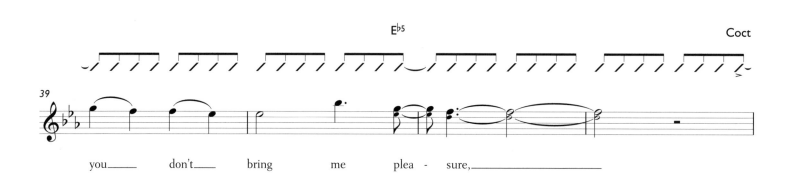

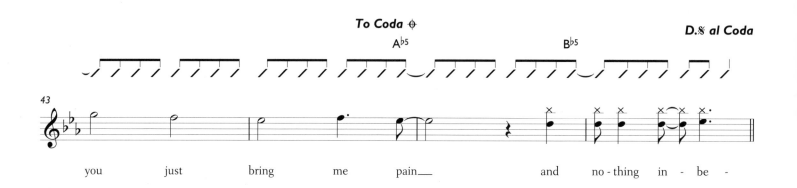

⊕ Coda

and no-thing in-be-tween,_____ no, no-thing in-be-tween.

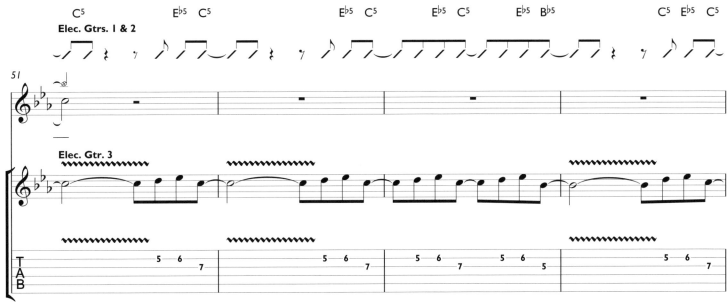

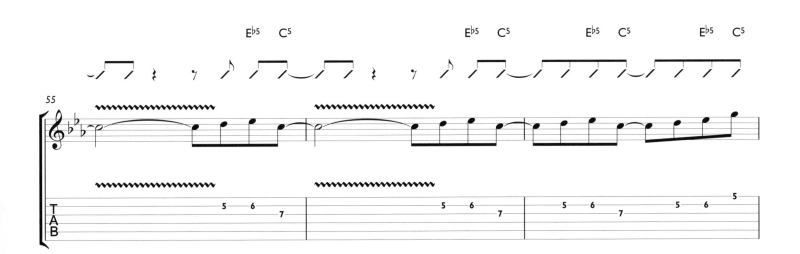

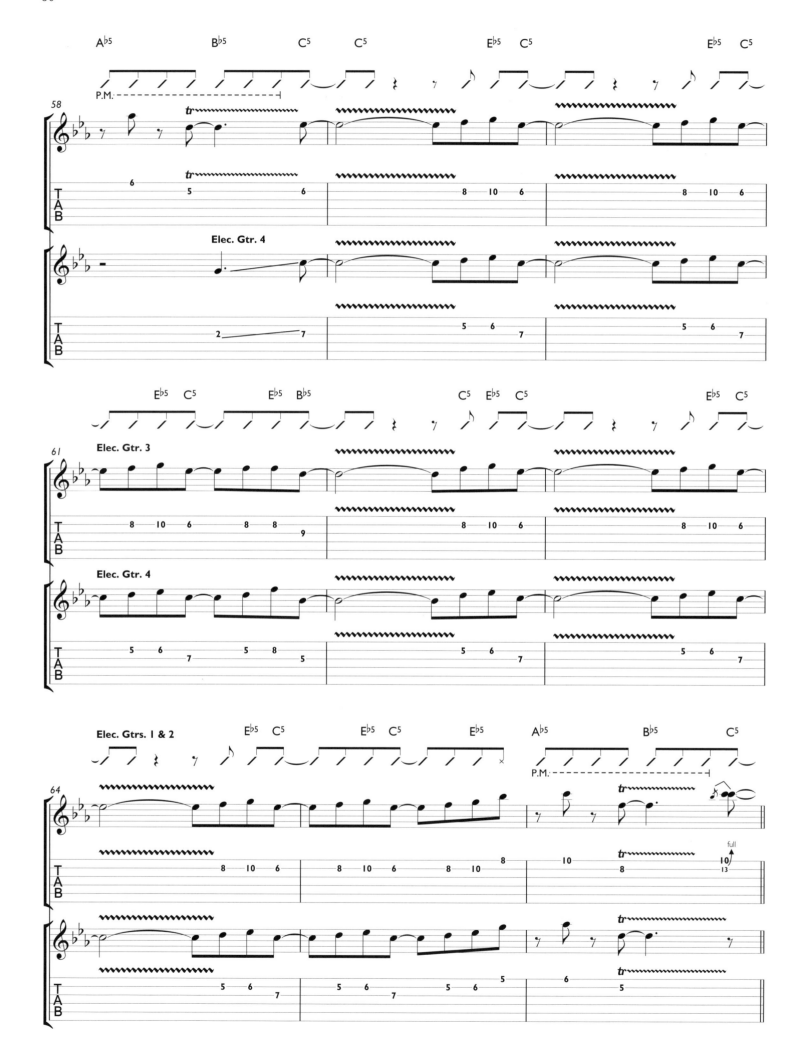

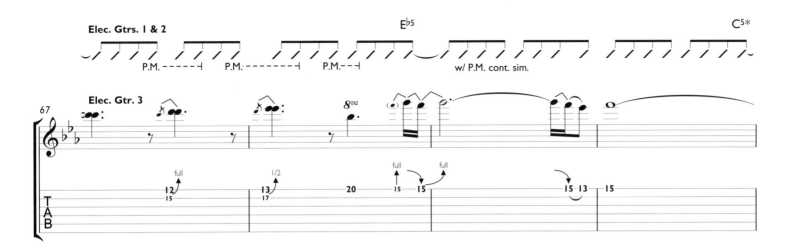

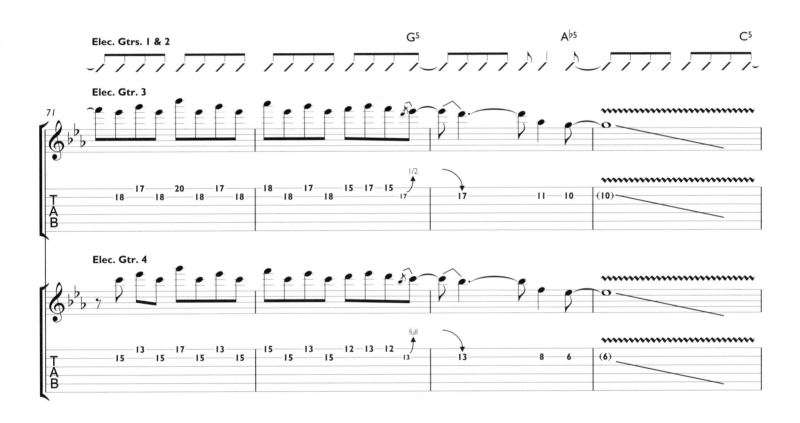

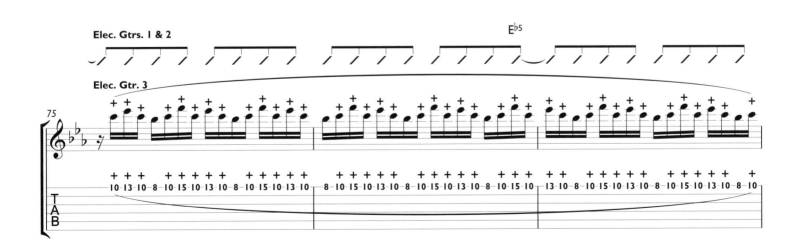

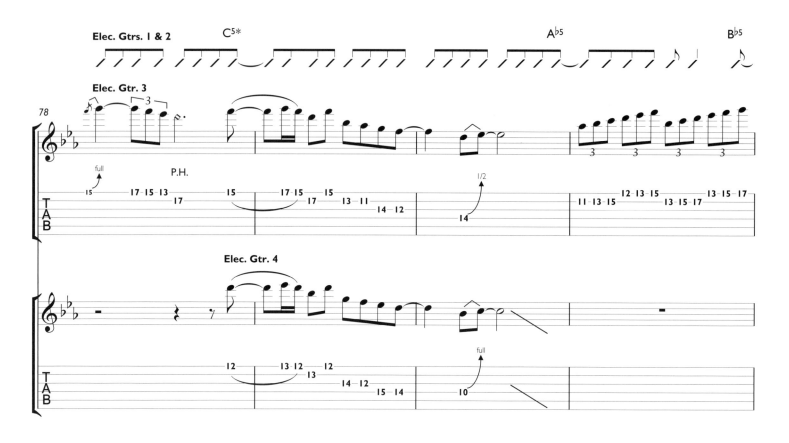

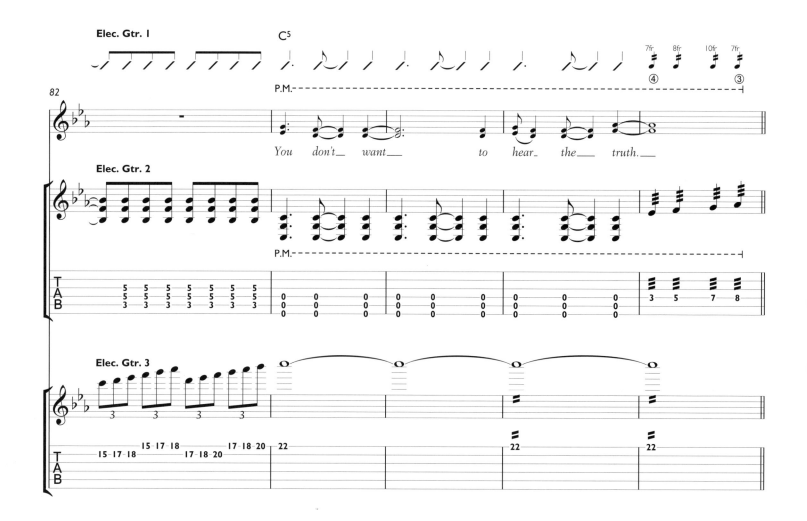

You don't__ want__ to hear_ the__ truth.__

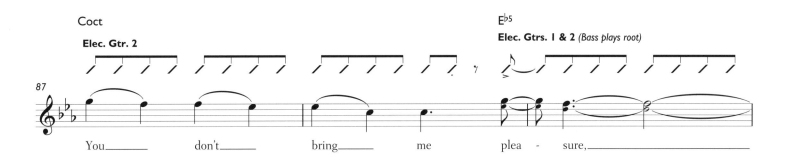

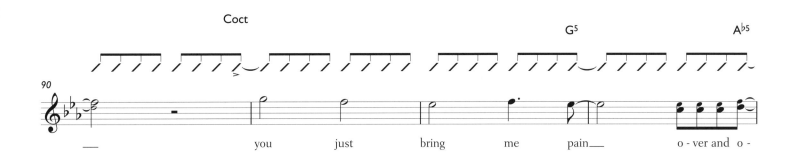

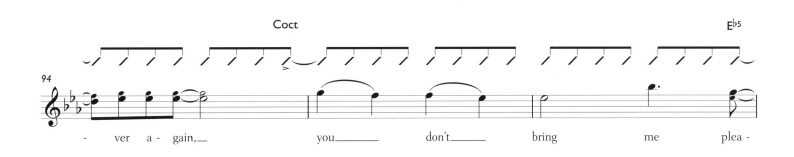

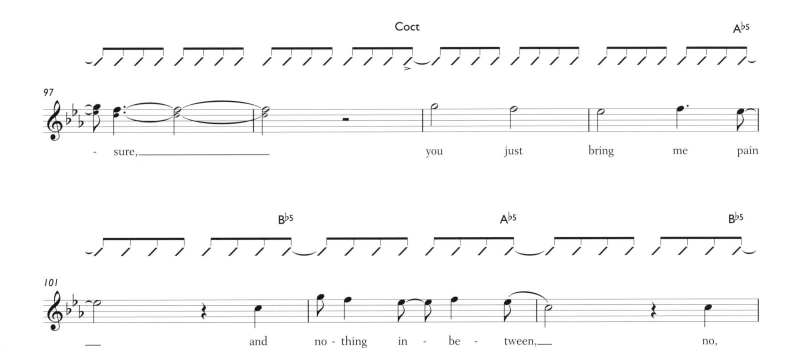

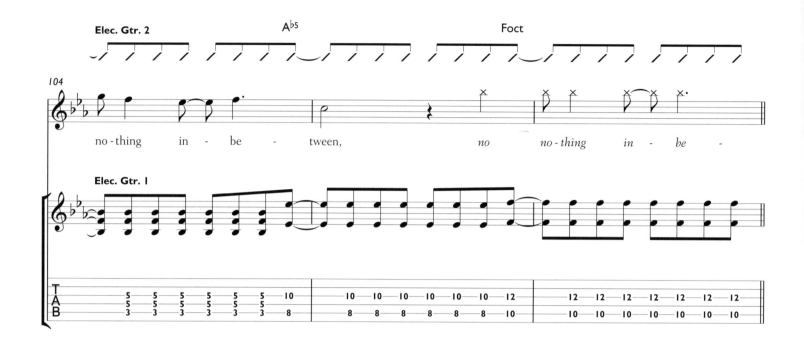

no-thing in - be - tween, no no-thing in - be -

- tween,_____ yeah.____
Elec. Gtrs. & Bass play Fig. 1   *Elec. Gtrs. & Bass play Fig. 1*

no, no-thing in - be - tween,
Elec. Gtrs. & Bass play Fig. 1

Elec. Gtrs. & Bass play Fig. 1   *Come take this sac - ri - fice!*

ALONE

Words and Music by Matthew Tuck, Jason James,
Michael Thomas and Michael Paget

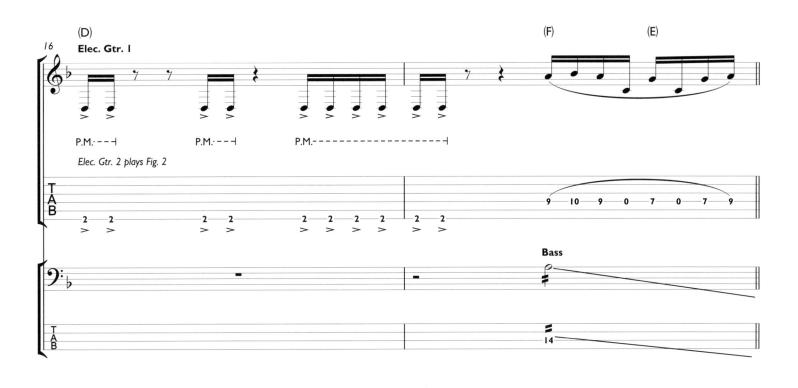

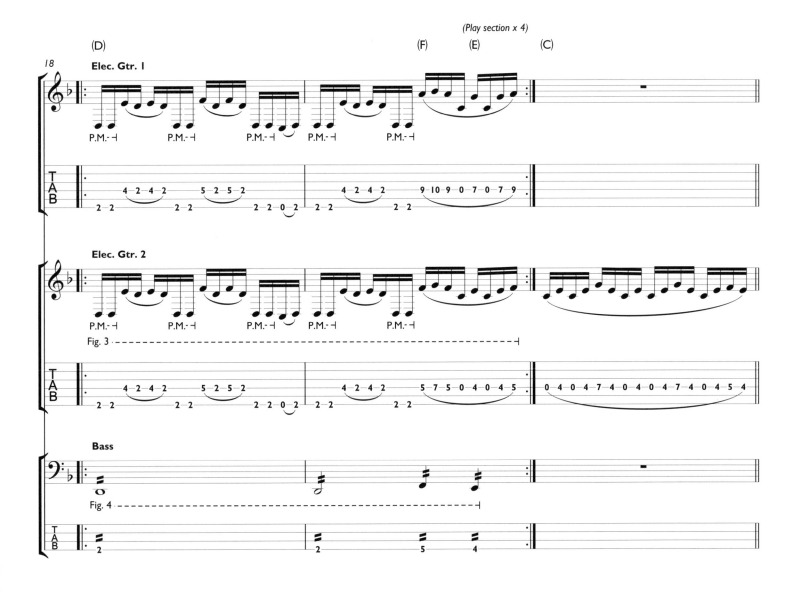

58

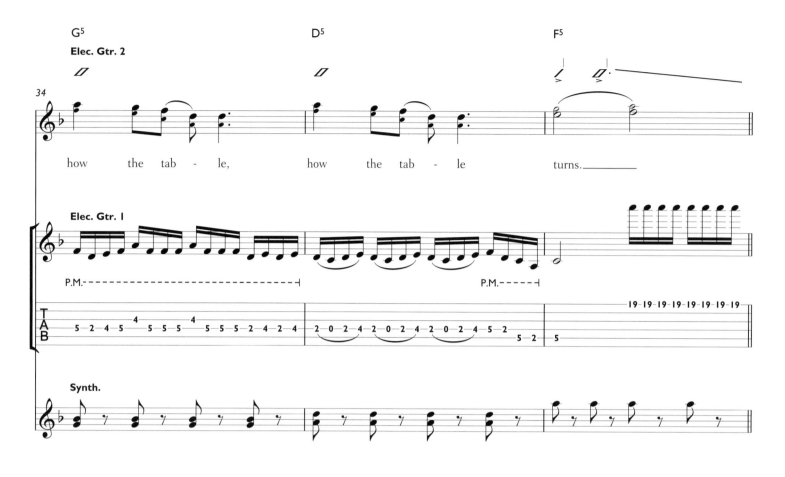

how the tab - le, how the tab - le turns.

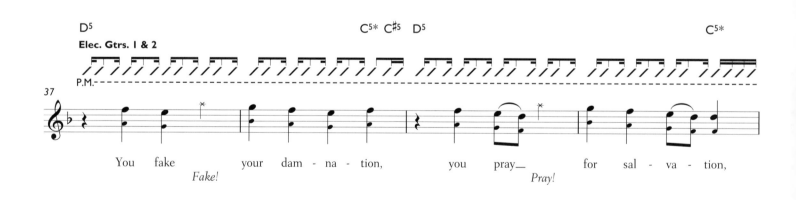

You fake your dam - na - tion, you pray for sal - va - tion,
Fake! *Pray!*

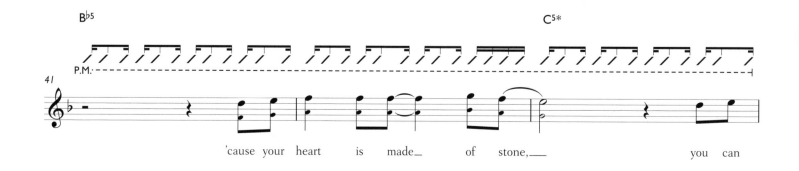

'cause your heart is made of stone, you can

62

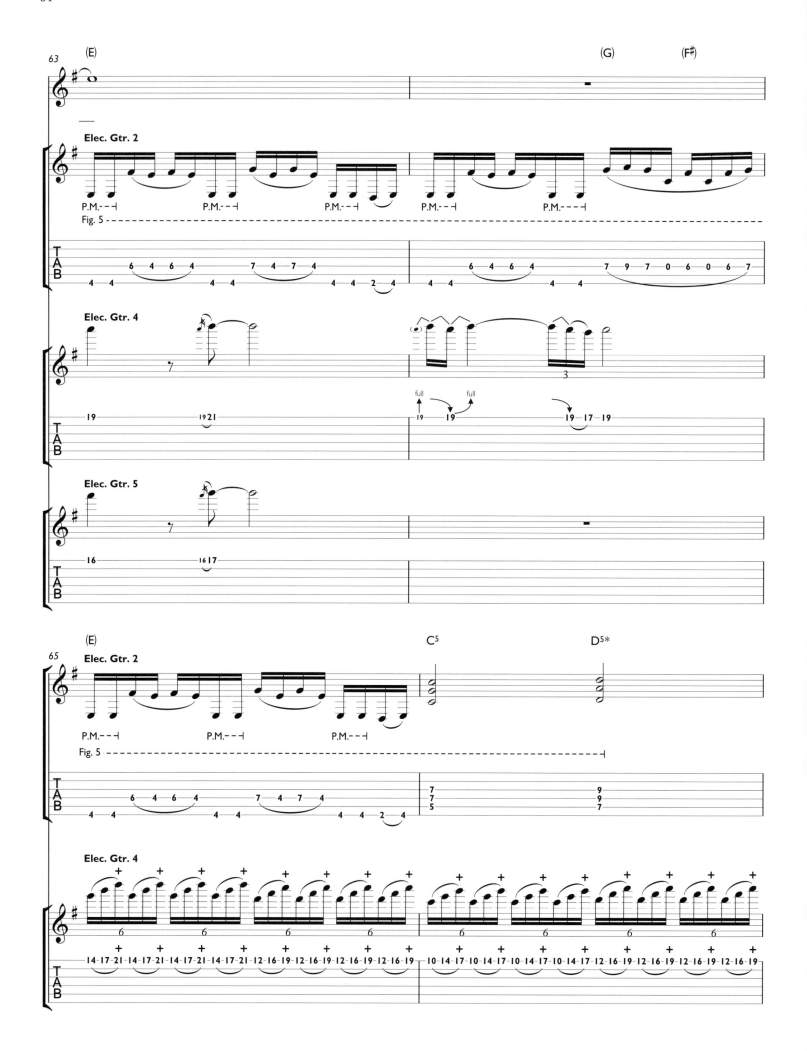

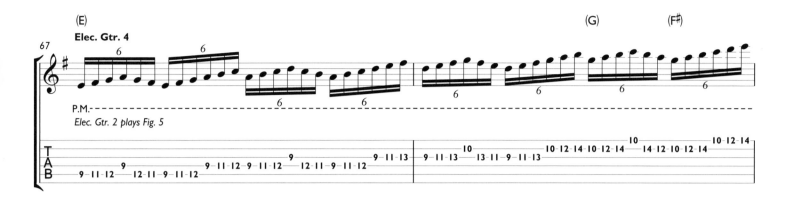

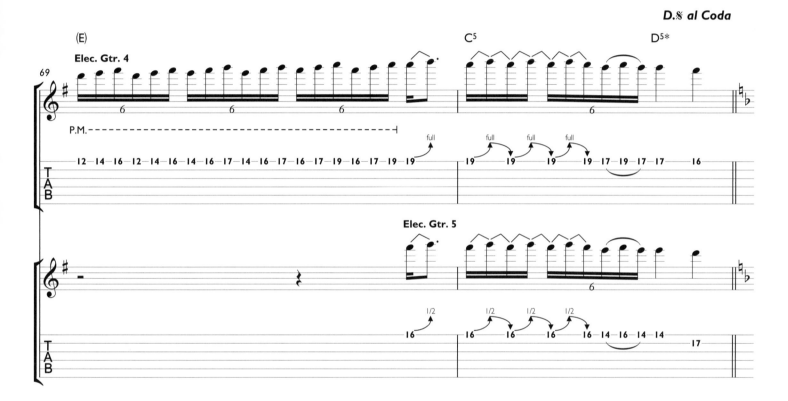

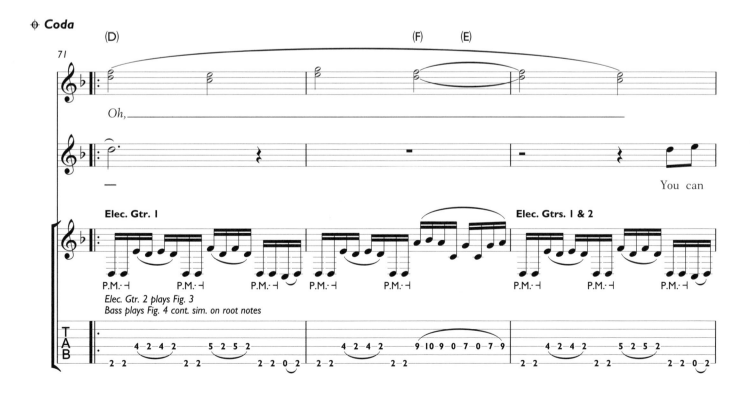

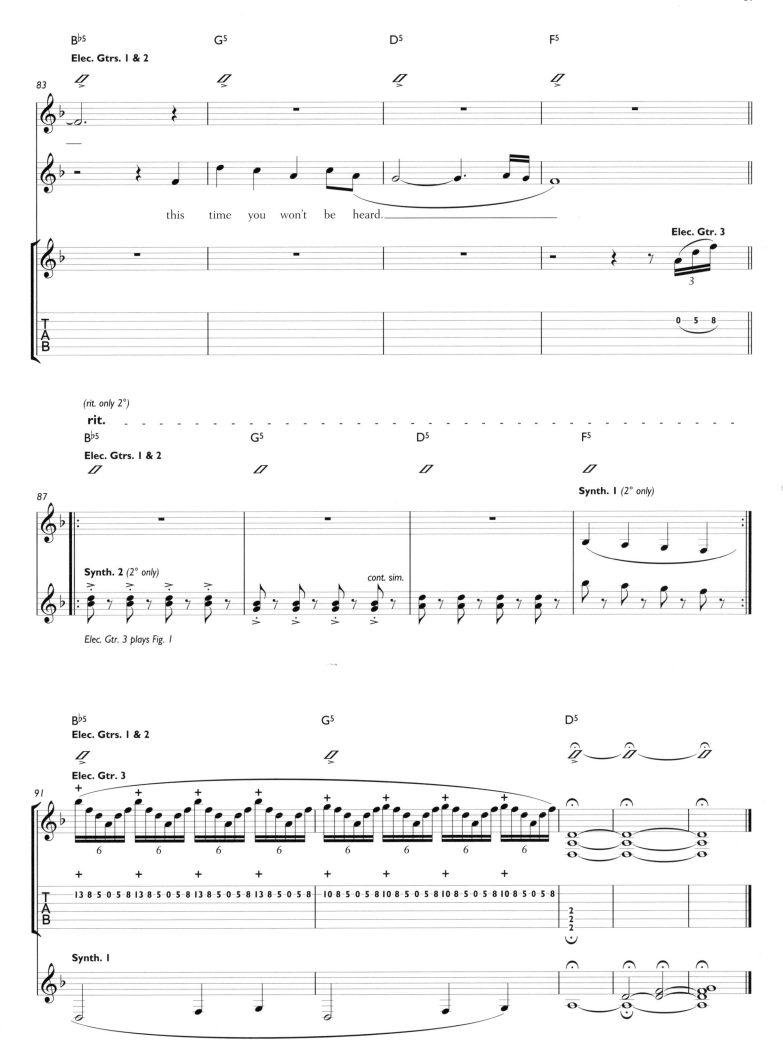

this time you won't be heard.

BREAKING OUT, BREAKING DOWN

Words and Music by Matthew Tuck, Jason James,
Michael Thomas and Michael Paget

Tune guitars:
1 = D 4 = C
2 = A 5 = G
3 = F 6 = low C

♩ = 176

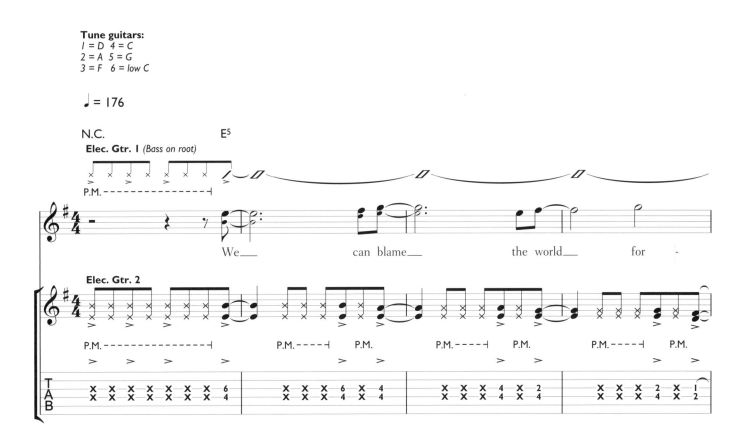

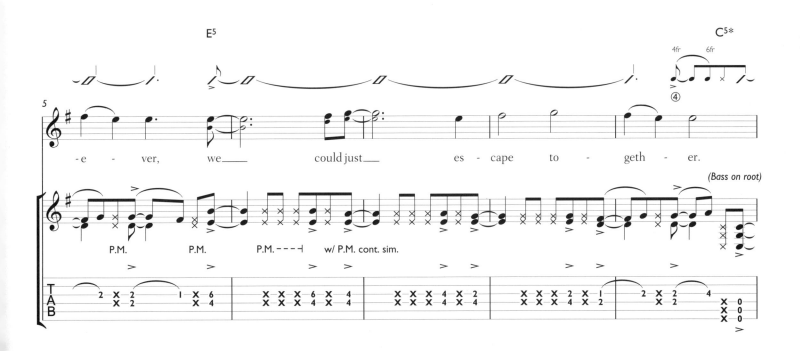

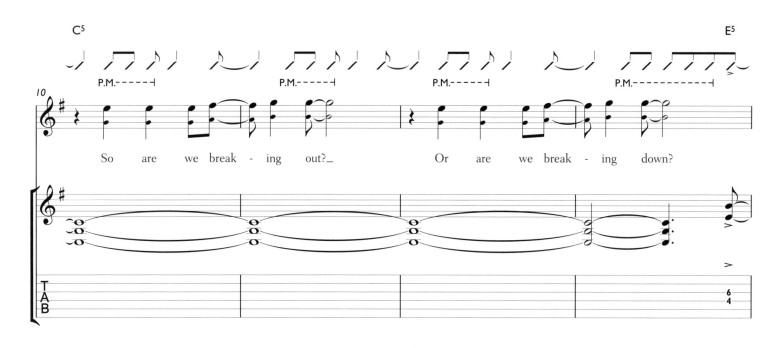

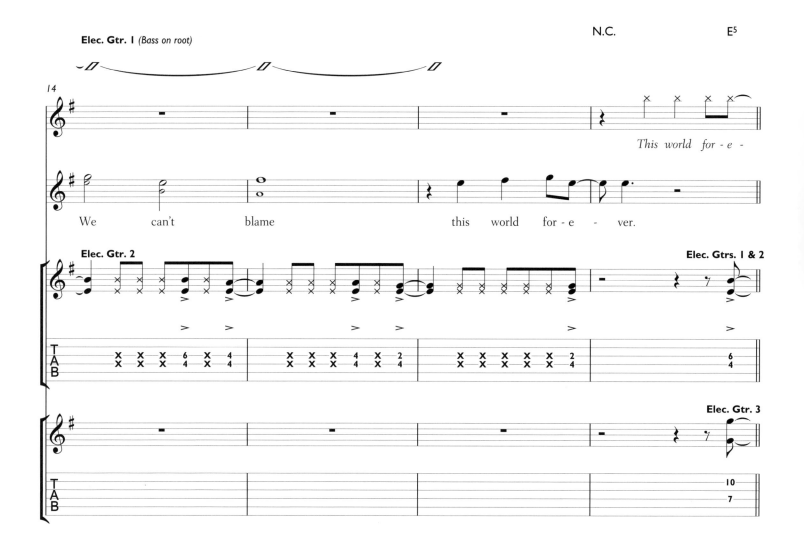

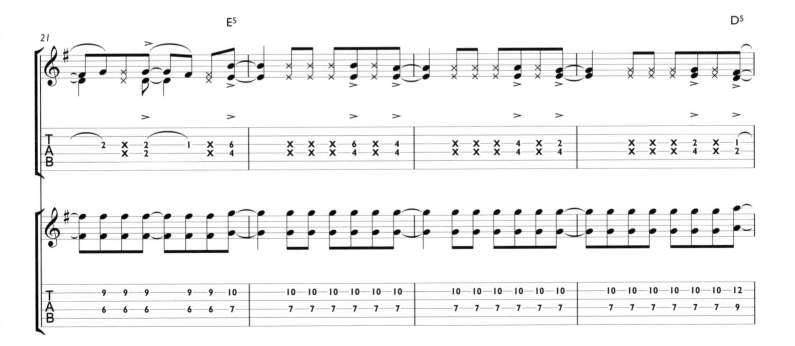

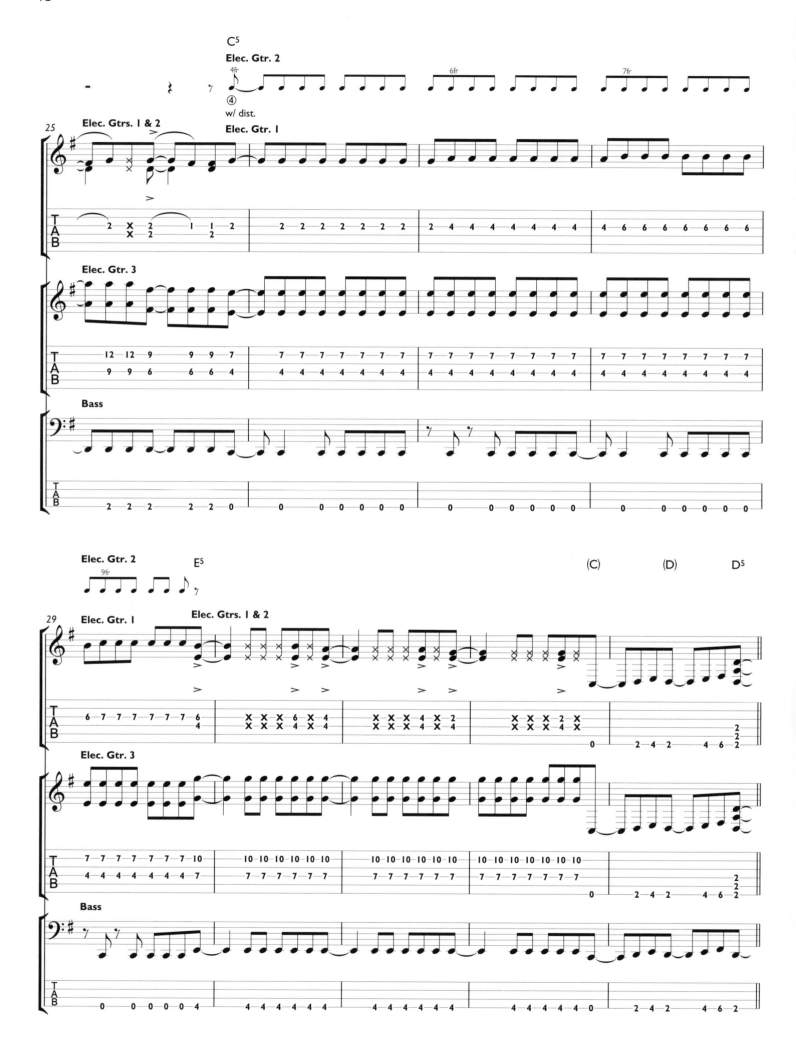

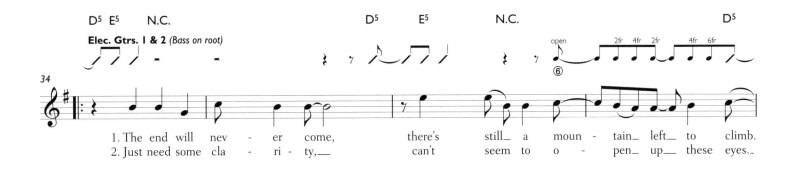

1. The end will nev - er come, there's still a moun - tain left to climb.
2. Just need some cla - ri - ty,__ can't seem to o - pen up these eyes.__

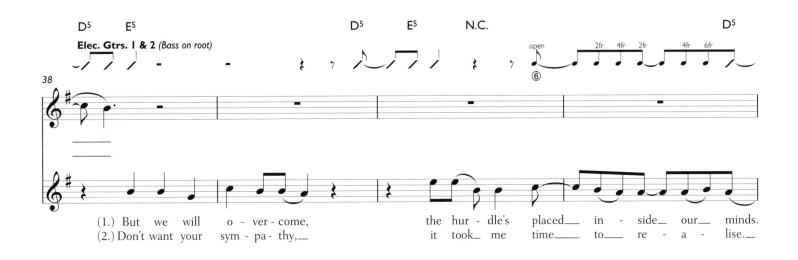

(1.) But we will o - ver - come, the hur - dle's placed__ in - side__ our__ minds.
(2.) Don't want your sym - pa - thy,__ it took__ me time__ to__ re - a - lise.__

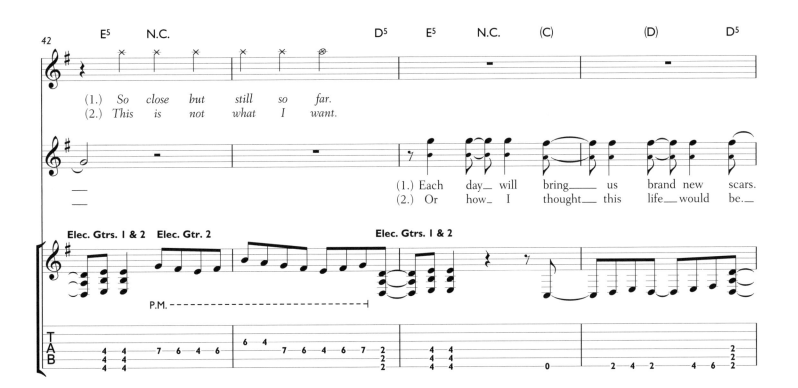

(1.) So close but still so far.
(2.) This is not what I want.

(1.) Each day__ will bring__ us brand new scars.
(2.) Or how__ I thought__ this life__ would be.__

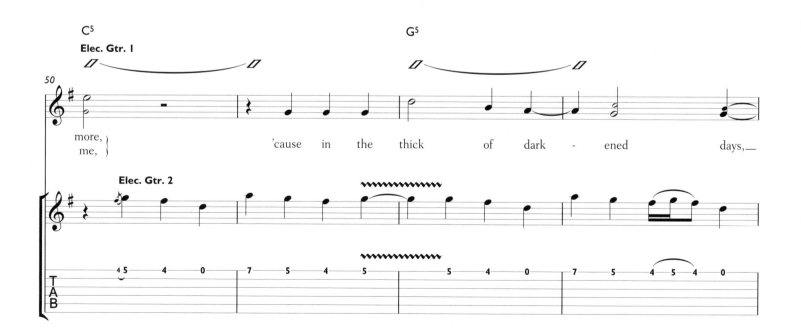

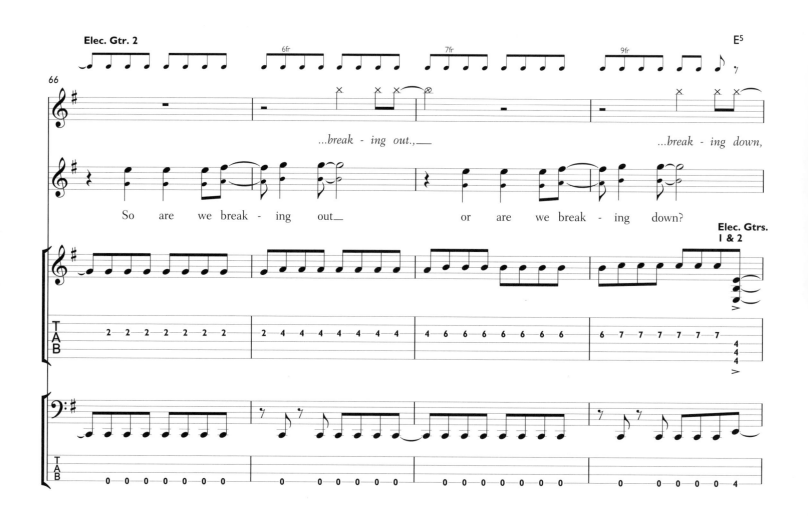

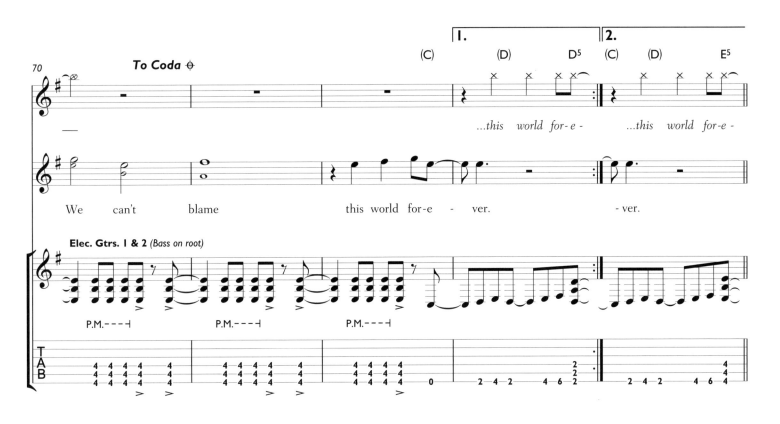

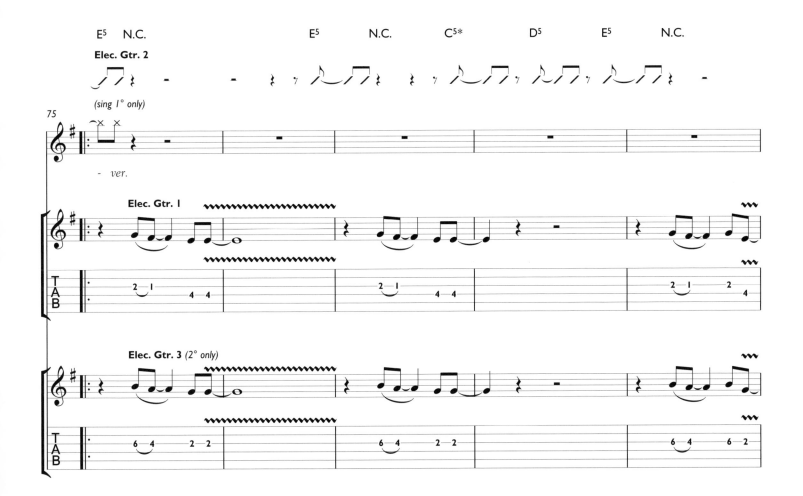

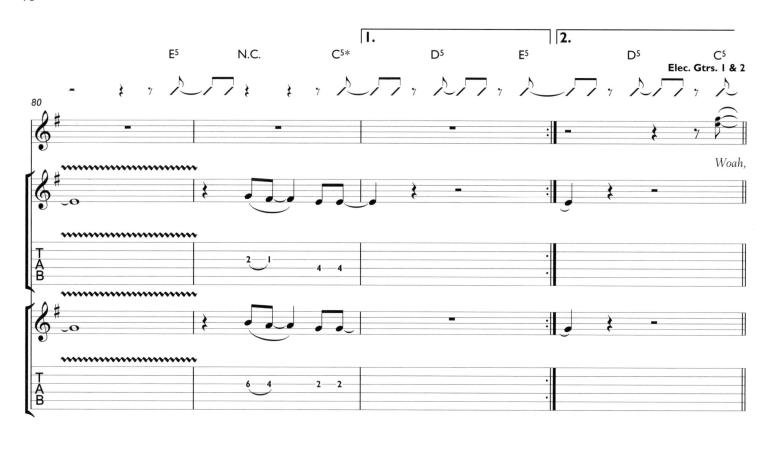

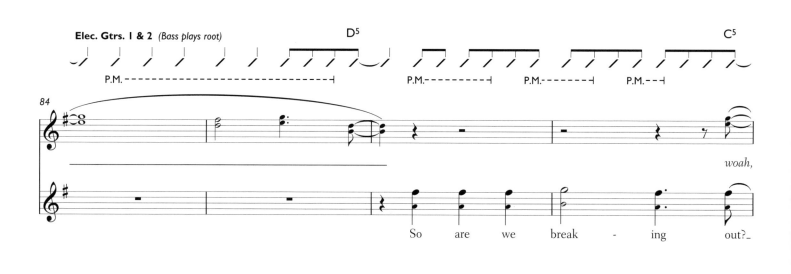

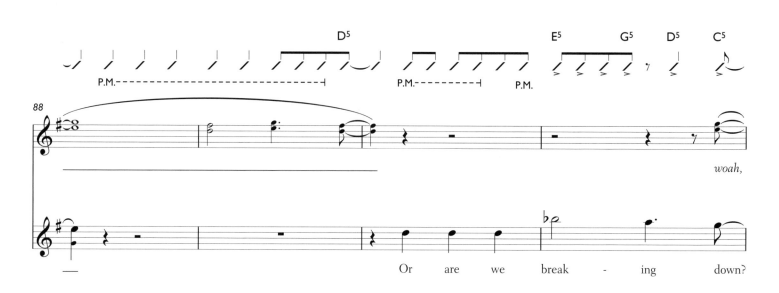

⊕ **Coda**

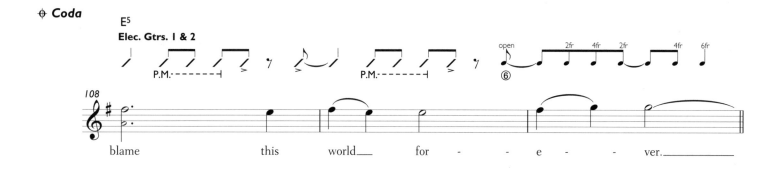

blame   this   world___   for   -   e   -   ver.___

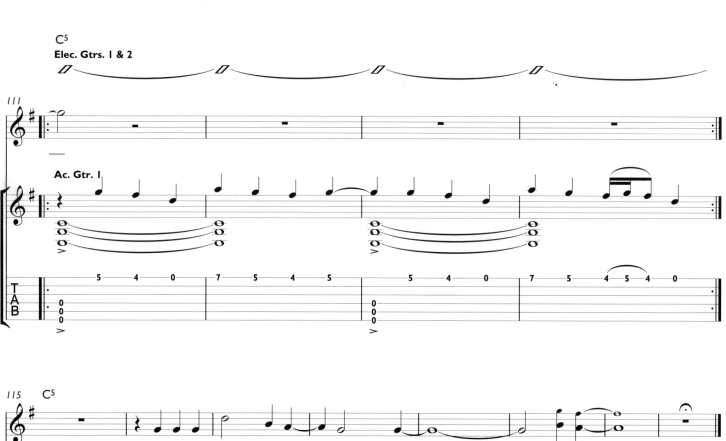

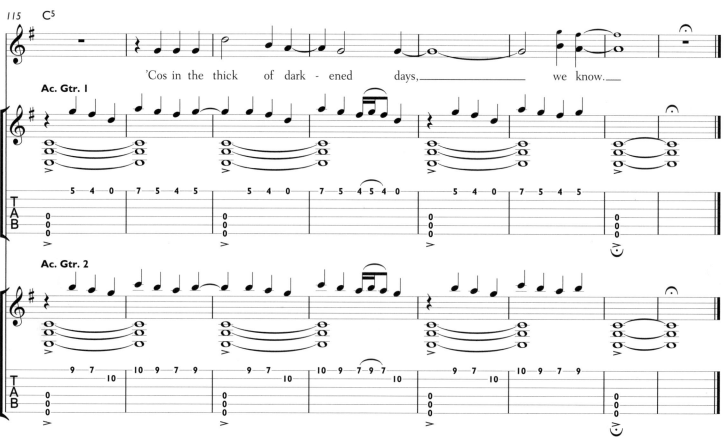

'Cos in the thick   of dark - ened   days,___   we know.___

BITTERSWEET MEMORIES

Words and Music by Matthew Tuck, Jason James, Michael Thomas and Michael Paget

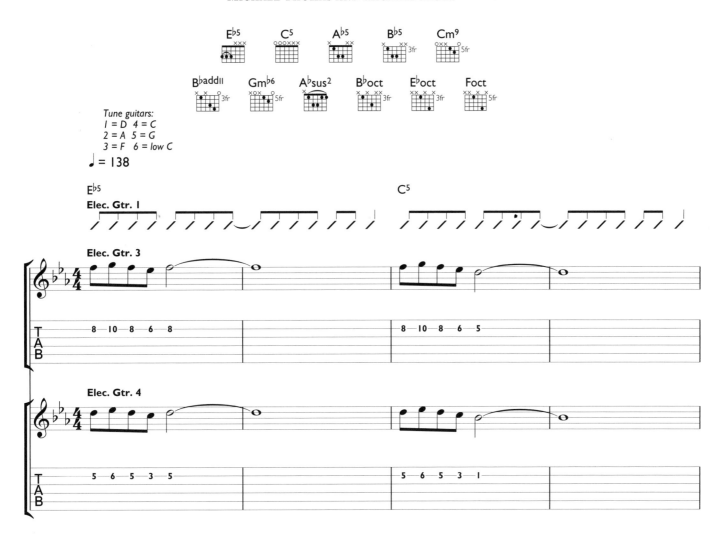

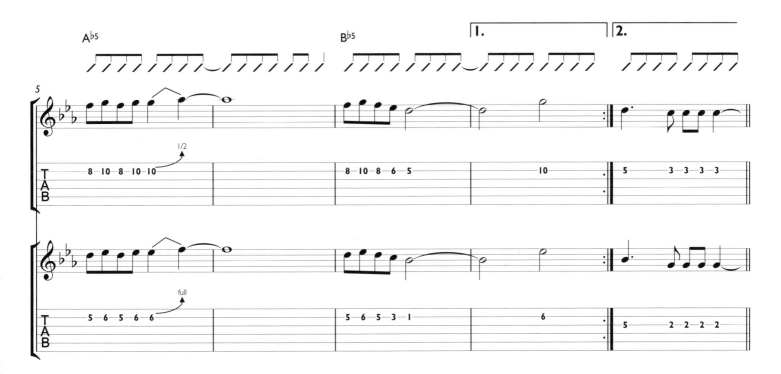

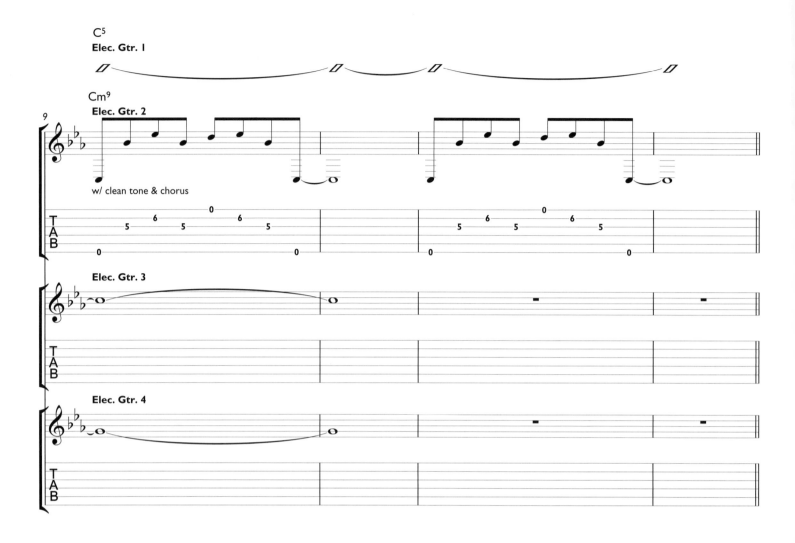

1. You turn me off___ at the push of a but-ton, and you pre-tend that I don't mean no - thing,
2. I wan-na run___ and es - cape from your pri-son, but when I leave, I feel some-thing is mis-sing,

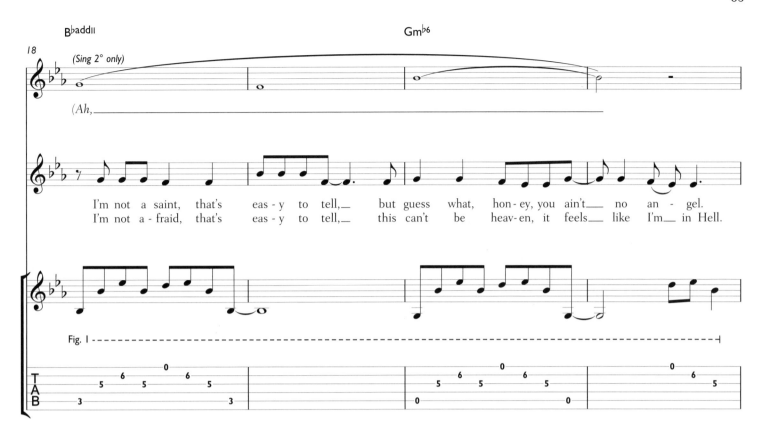

I'm not a saint, that's eas-y to tell,___ but guess what, hon-ey, you ain't___ no an - gel.
I'm not a-fraid, that's eas-y to tell,___ this can't be heav-en, it feels___ like I'm___ in Hell.

You like to scream use words as a wea-pon, well go a-head, take your best shot,___ wo-man.
You're like a drug___ that I can't stop___ tak-ing, I want___ more and I can't stop___ crav-ing,

Elec. Gtr. 2 plays Fig. 1

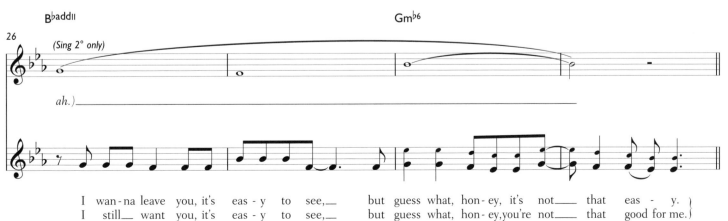

I wan-na leave you, it's eas-y to see,___ but guess what, hon-ey, it's not___ that eas - y.)
I still___ want you, it's eas-y to see,___ but guess what, hon-ey, you're not___ that good for me.)

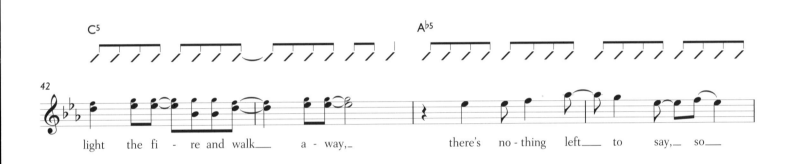

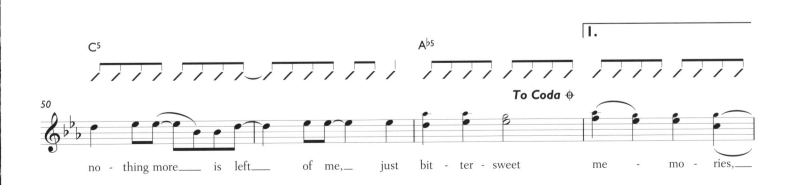

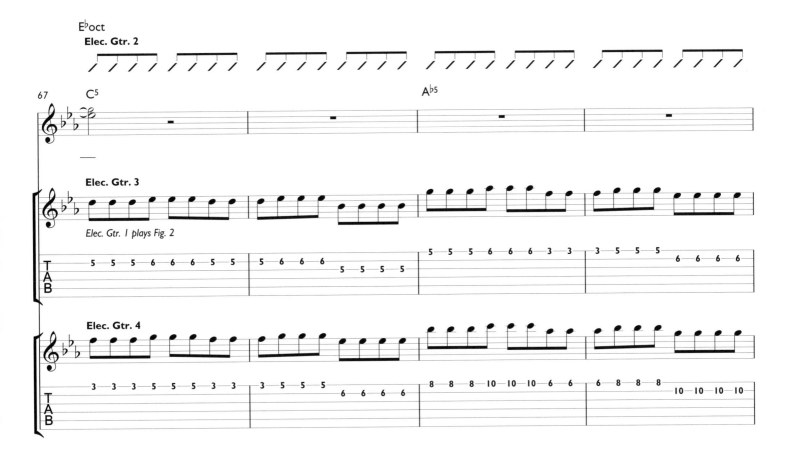

So

com - pli - cat - ed._____

So

⊕ *Coda*

Woah,_____

woah,

me - mo - ries,_____

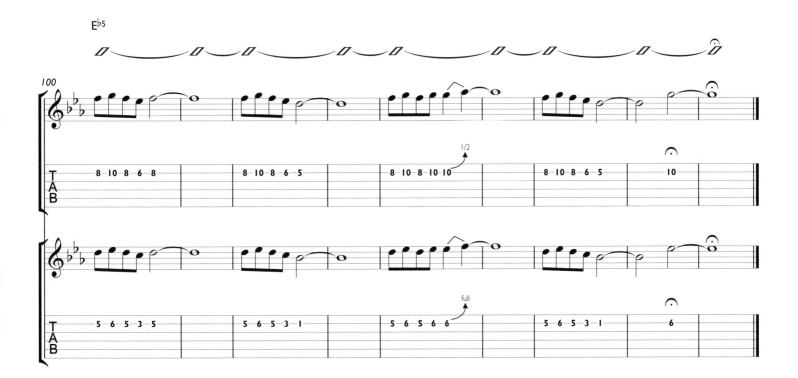

DIGNITY

Words and Music by Matthew Tuck, Jason James,
Michael Thomas and Michael Paget

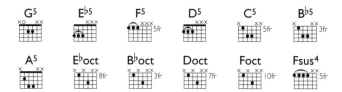

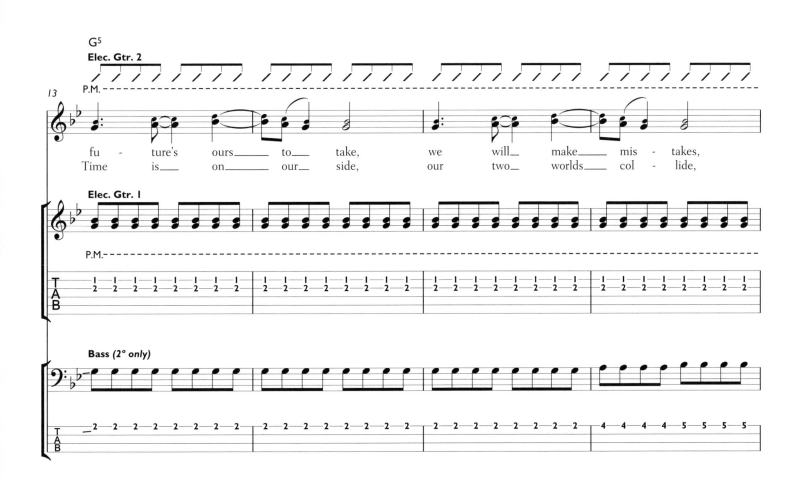

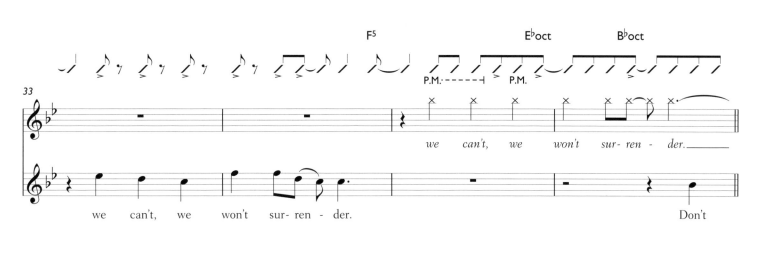

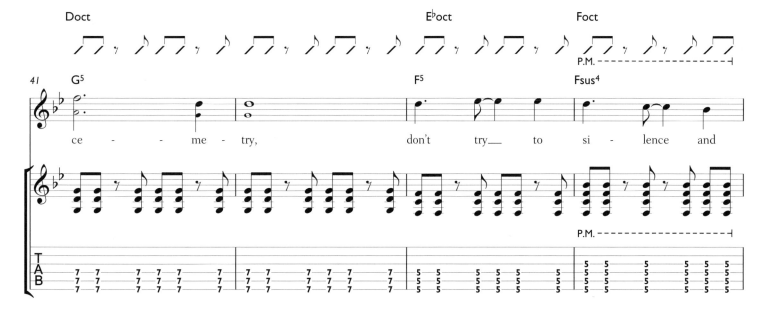

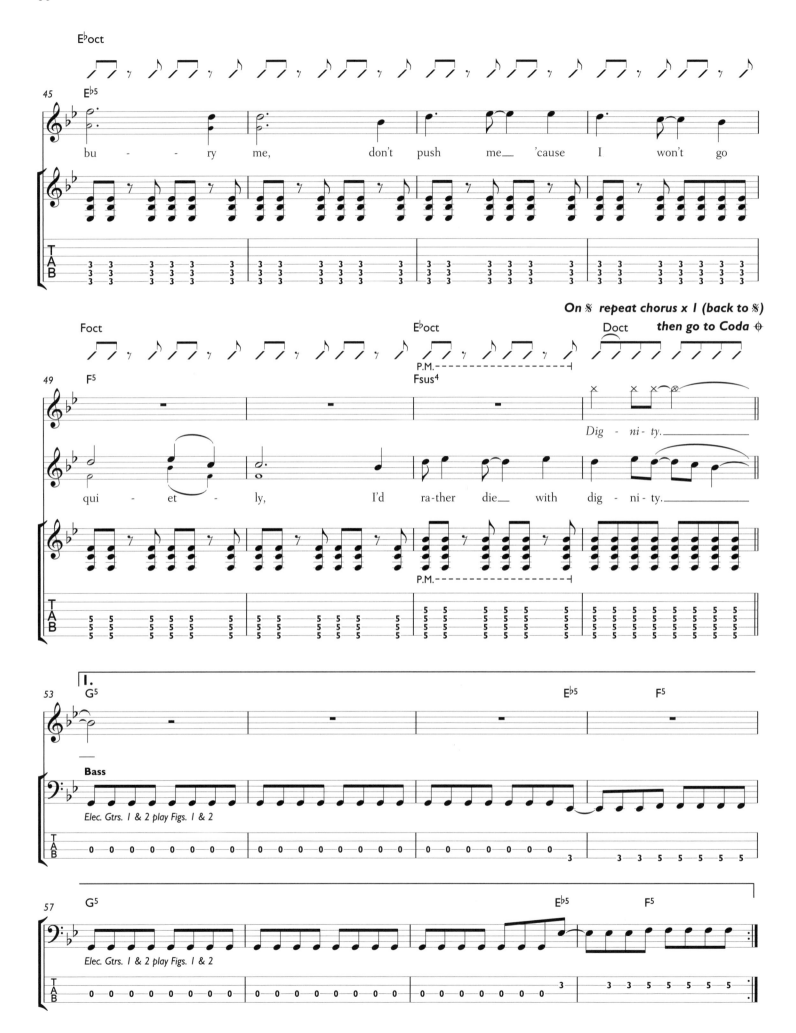

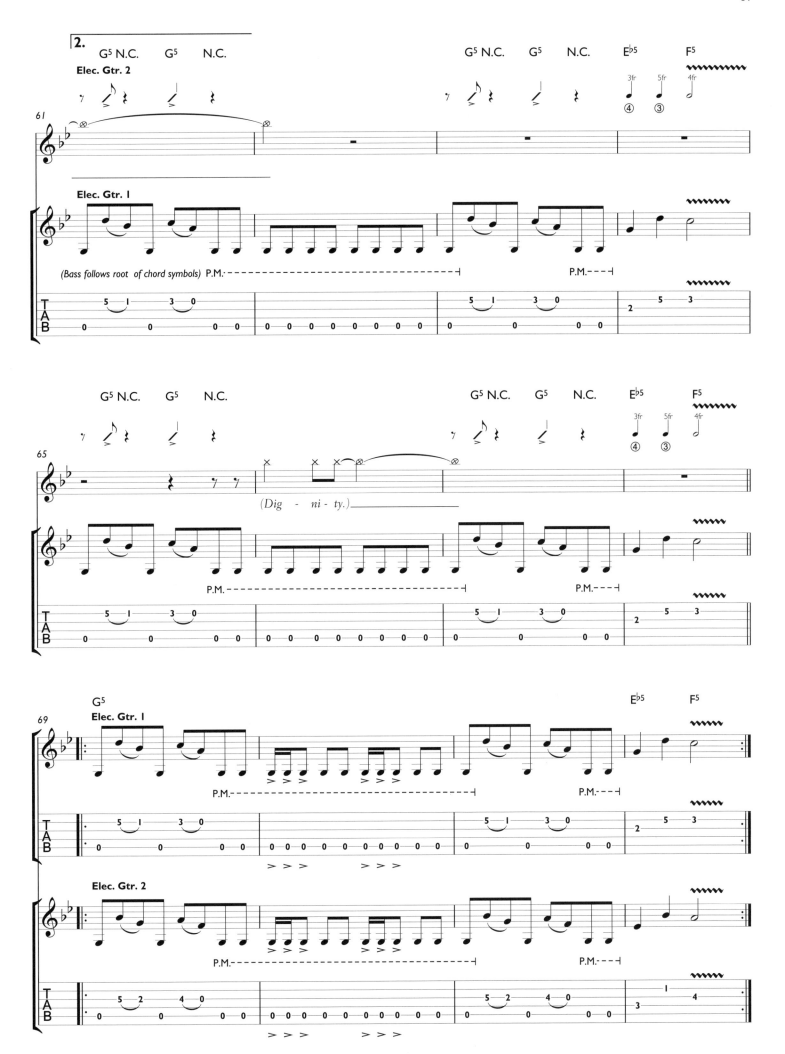

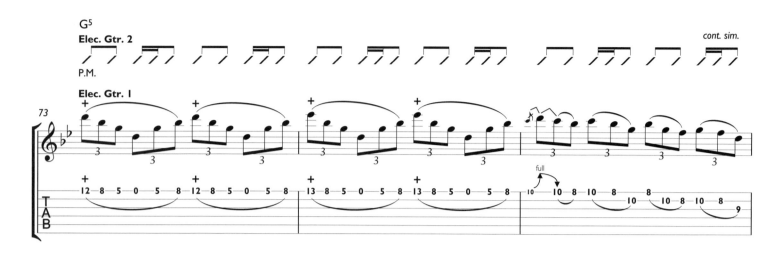

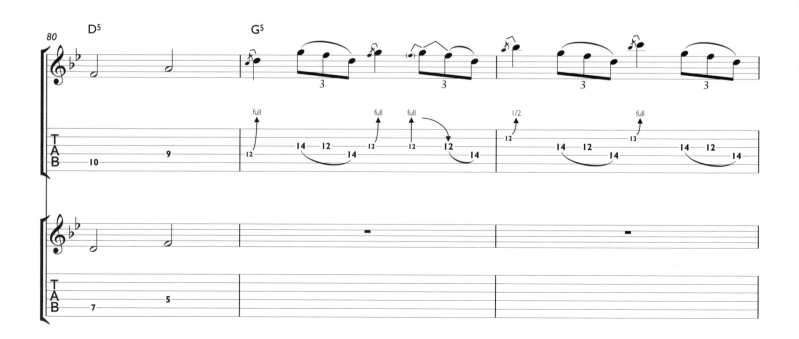

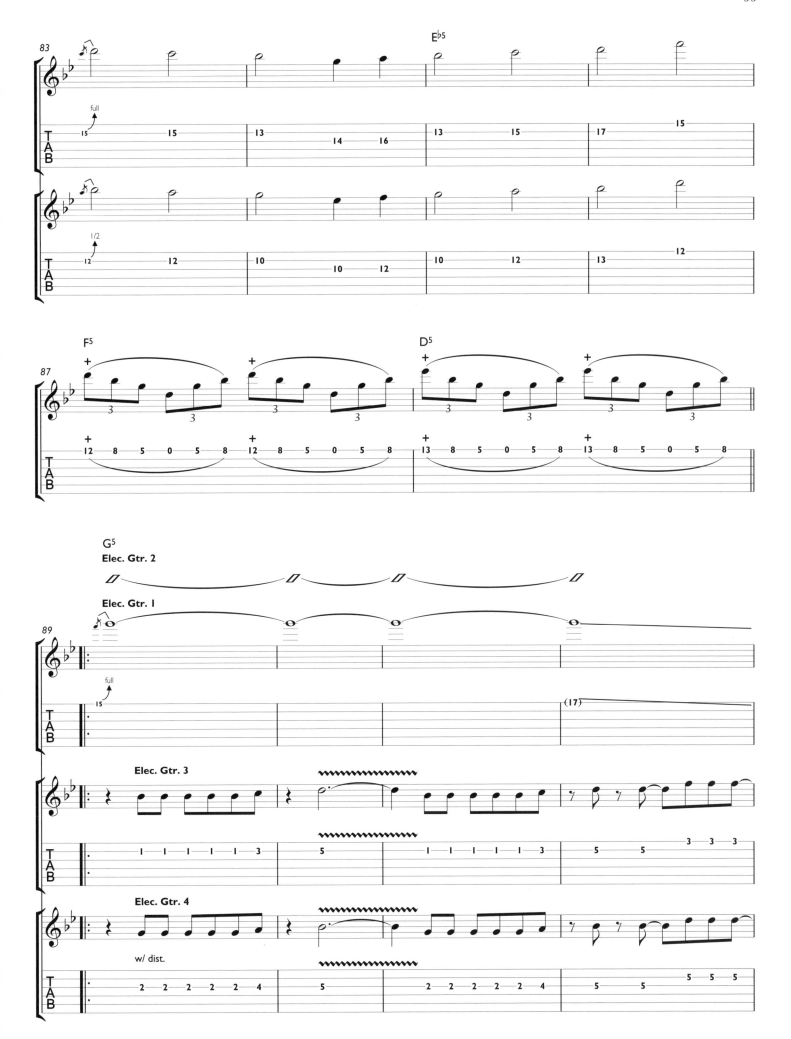

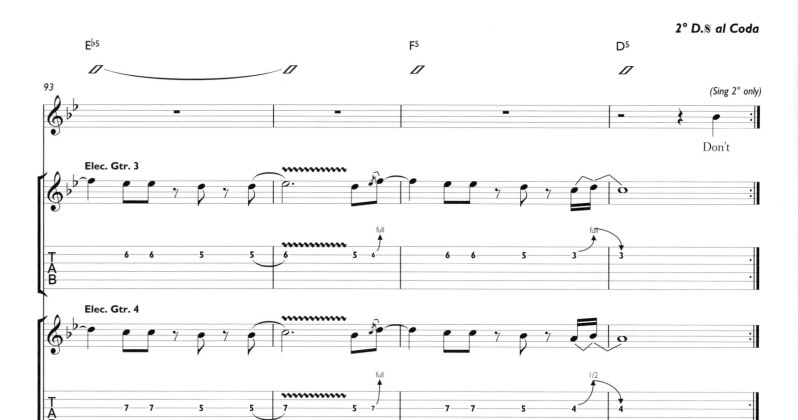

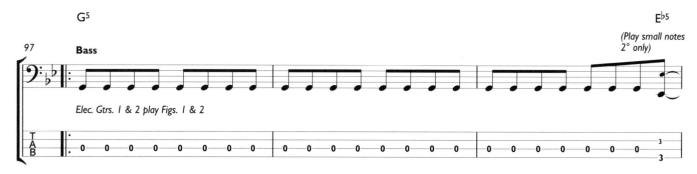

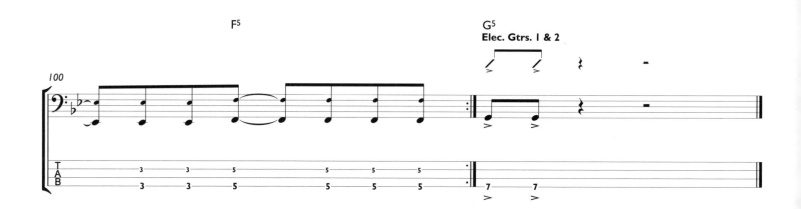

BEGGING FOR MERCY

Words and Music by Matthew Tuck, Jason James, Michael Thomas and Michael Paget

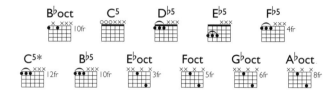

Tune guitars:
1 = D 4 = C
2 = A 5 = G
3 = F 6 = low C

♩ = 168

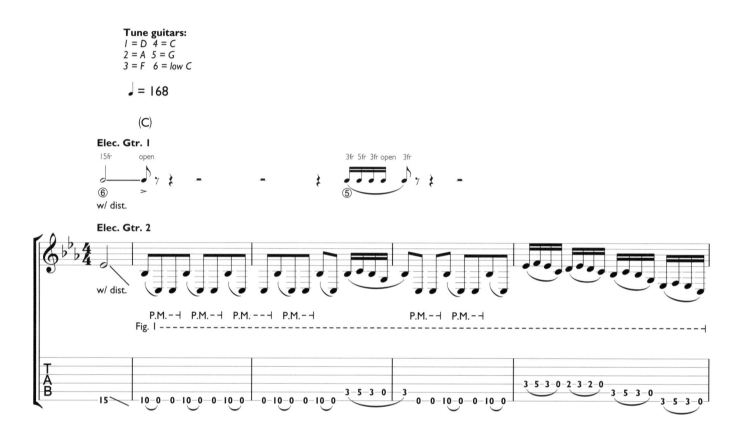

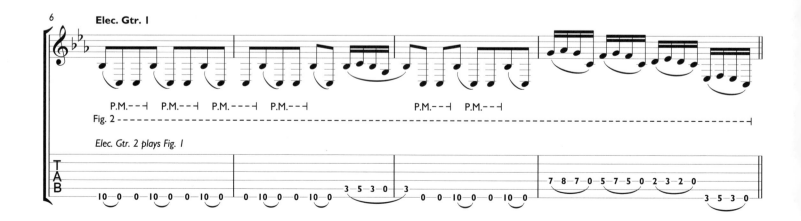

104

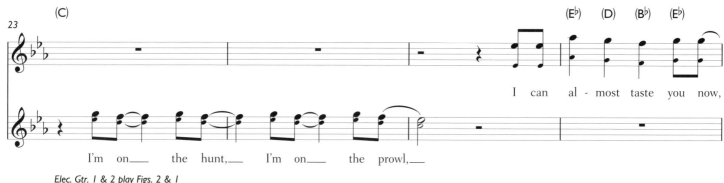

Elec. Gtr. 1 & 2 play Figs. 2 & 1
Bass plays Fig. 3

Elec. Gtr. 1 & 2 play Figs. 2 & 1
Bass plays Fig. 3

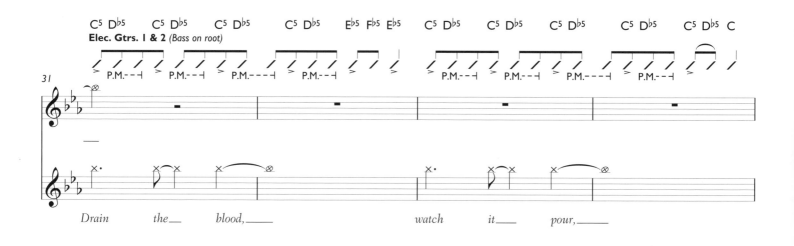

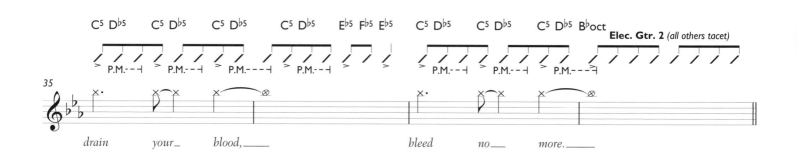

Drain   your___ blood,_____   watch   it___ pour,___

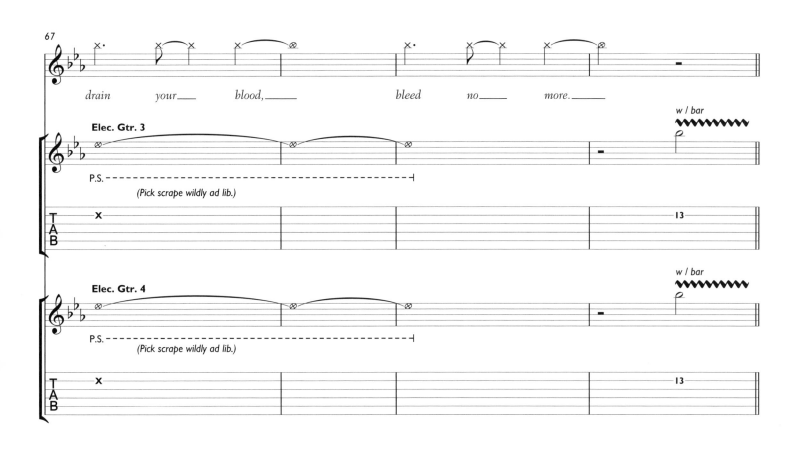

drain   your___   blood,___   bleed   no___   more.___

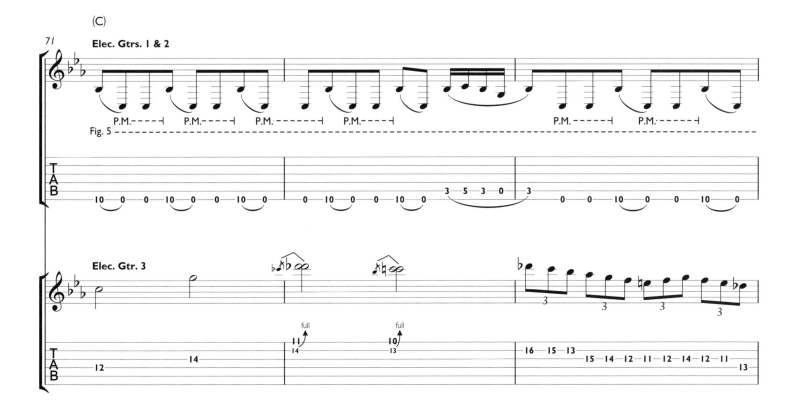

108

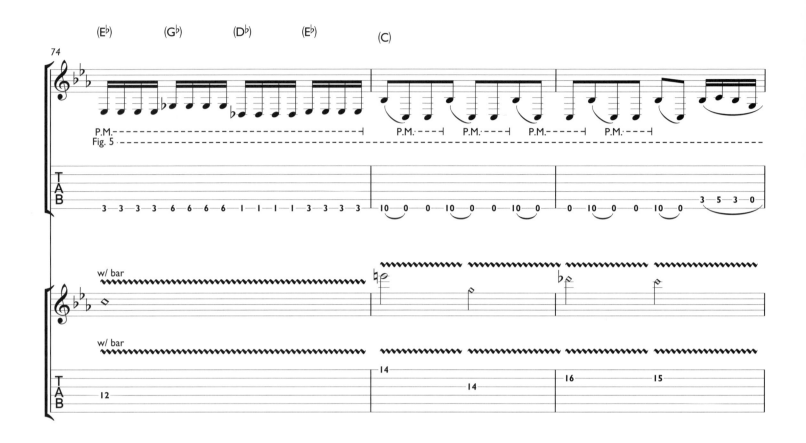

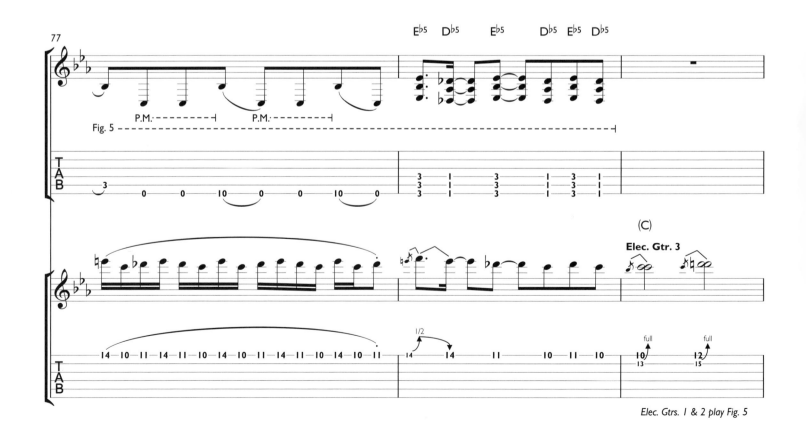

Elec. Gtrs. 1 & 2 play Fig. 5

110

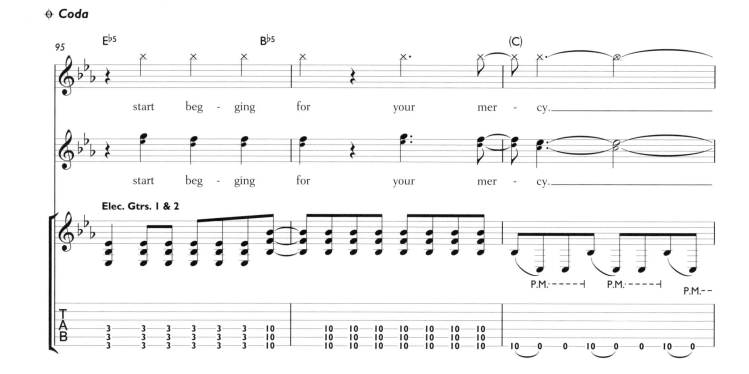

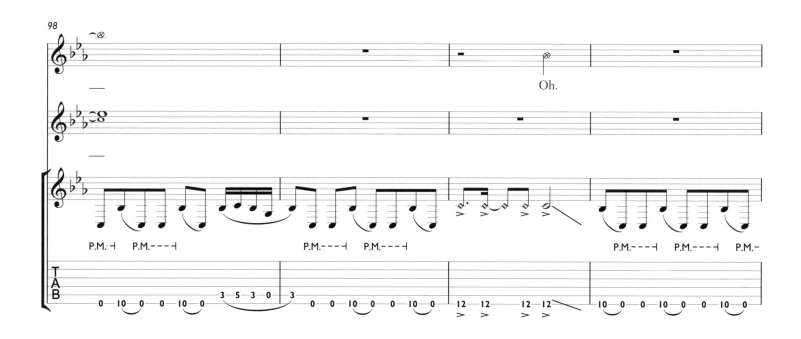

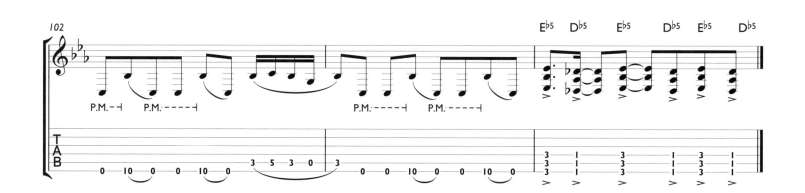

PRETTY ON THE OUTSIDE

Words and Music by Matthew Tuck, Jason James,
Michael Thomas and Michael Paget

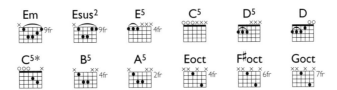

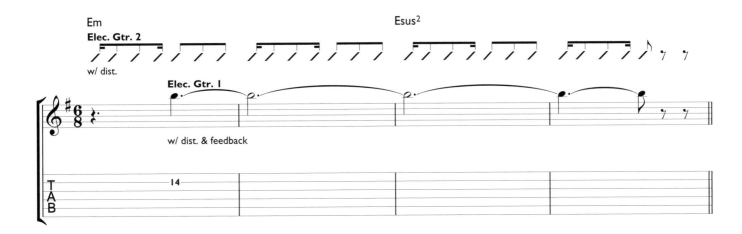

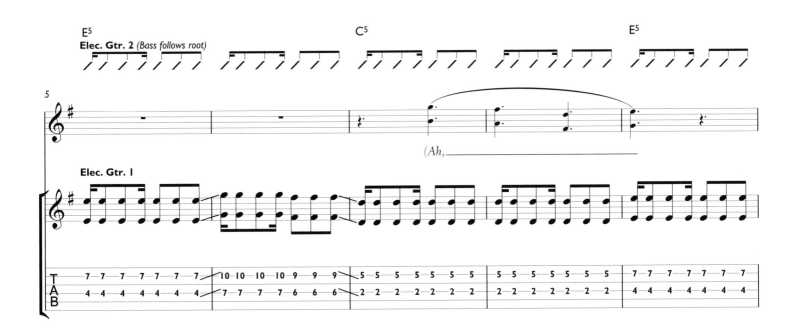

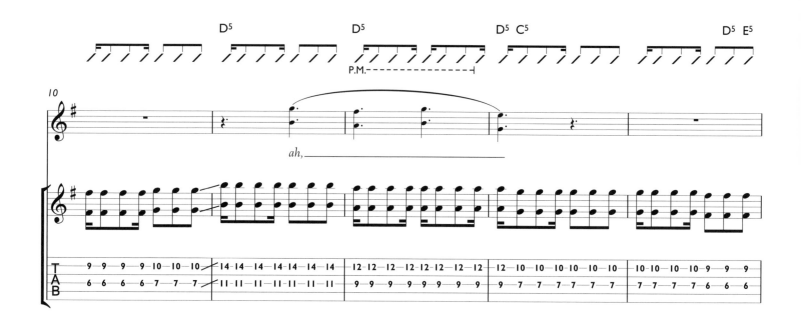

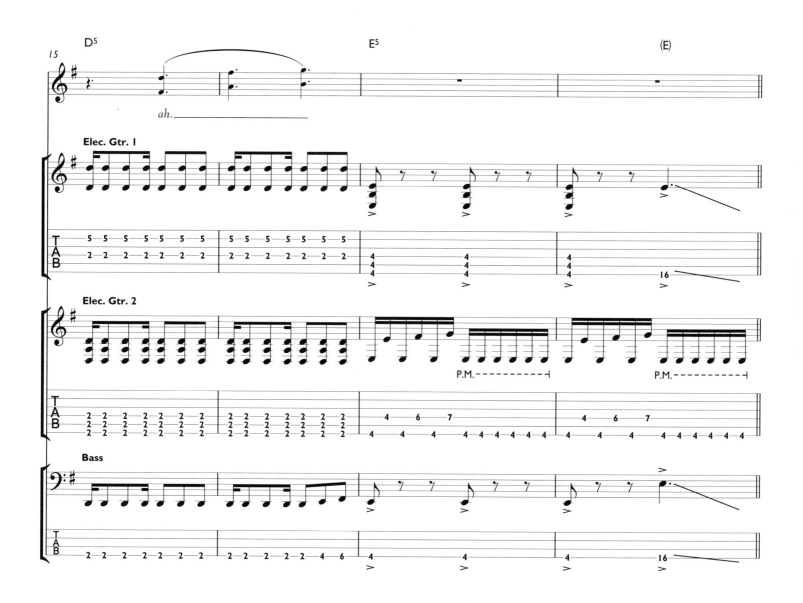

cloud._____ All the ne - ga - ti - vi - ty for - ces me down in - to si - lence, but still I can

Elec. Gtr. 1 plays Fig. 2
Elec. Gtr. 2 plays Fig. 1

dream.   I wan - na   know,   *I   wan - na   know   if   I*
low.   I wan - na   know,   *I   wan - na   know   if   I*

Elec. Gtrs. 1 & 2

Elec. Gtr. 2 *(Bass follows root)*

tear   you o - pen wide,   take   a   look in - side, are   you   pret - ty,

Elec. Gtr. 1

can   I   get in - side your mind,   see   what I   can find, are   you

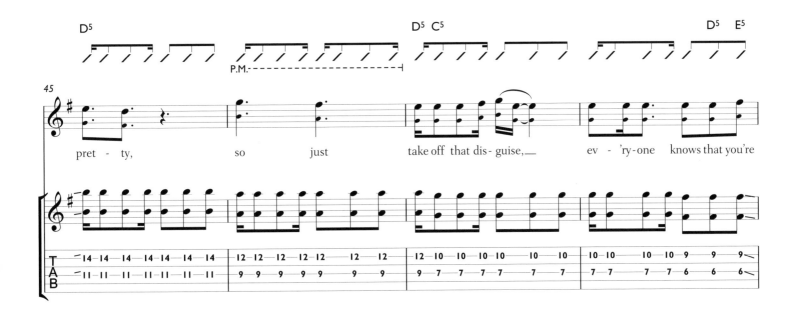

pret - ty,   so   just   take off that dis- guise,___   ev - 'ry-one   knows that you're

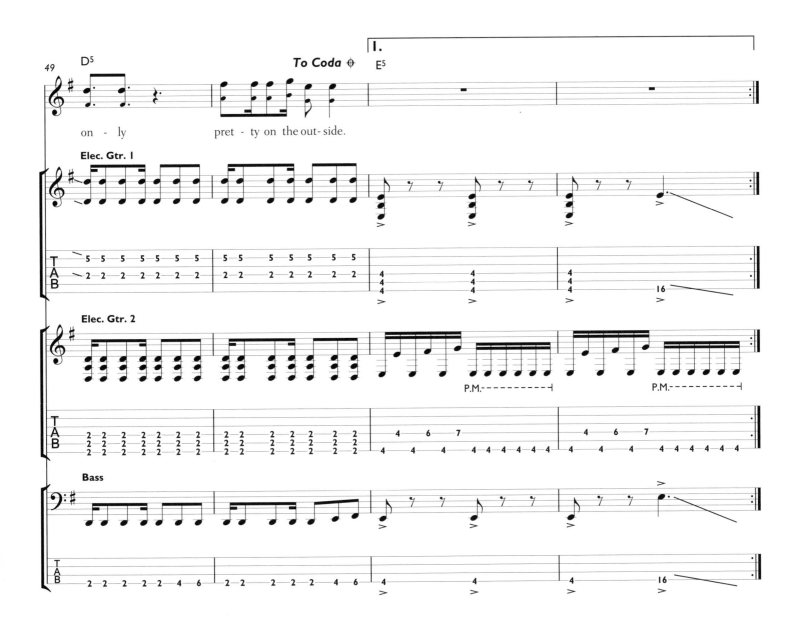

on - ly   pret - ty on the out- side.

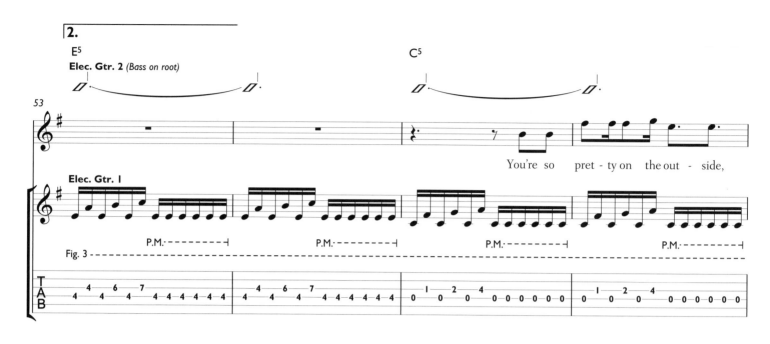

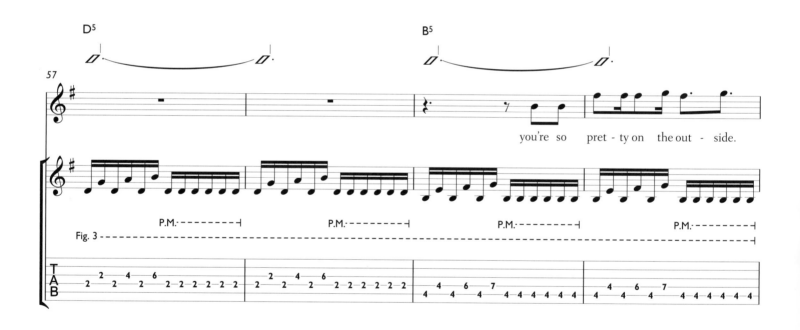

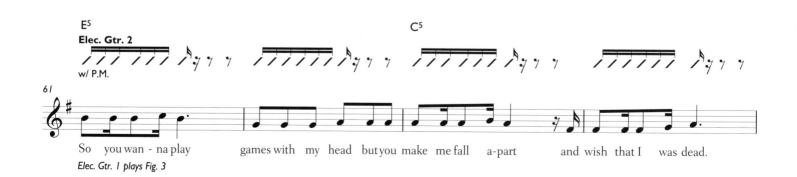

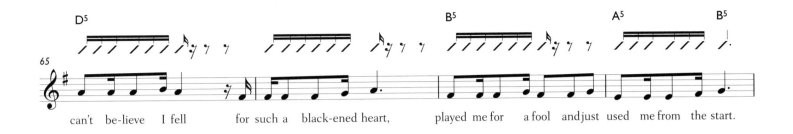

can't be-lieve I fell for such a black-ened heart, played me for a fool and just used me from the start.

but the words from your mouth, you keep

I just wan-na know the truth, all your ne-ga-ti-vi-ty,

for-cing me down, in-to si-lence I can dream.

in-to si-lence I can dream, in-to si-lence I can dream.

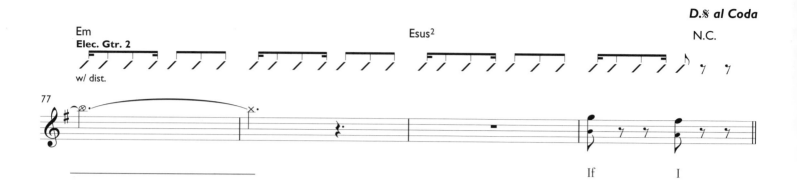

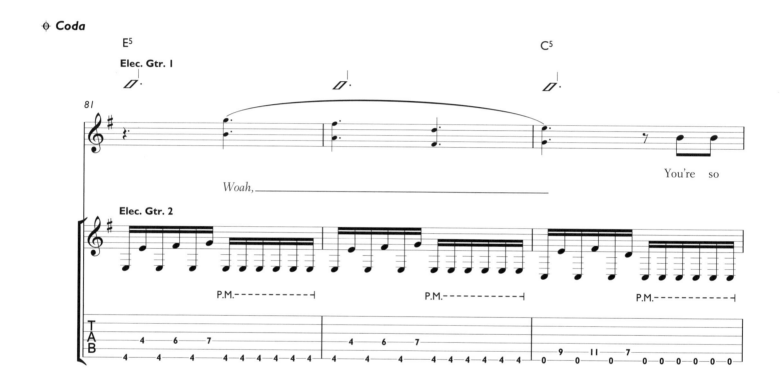

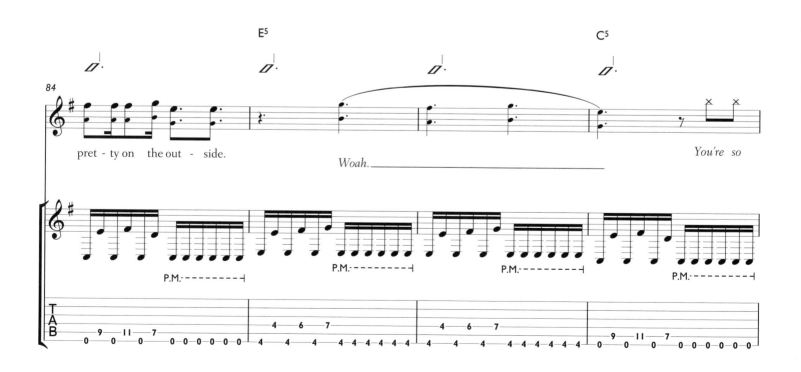

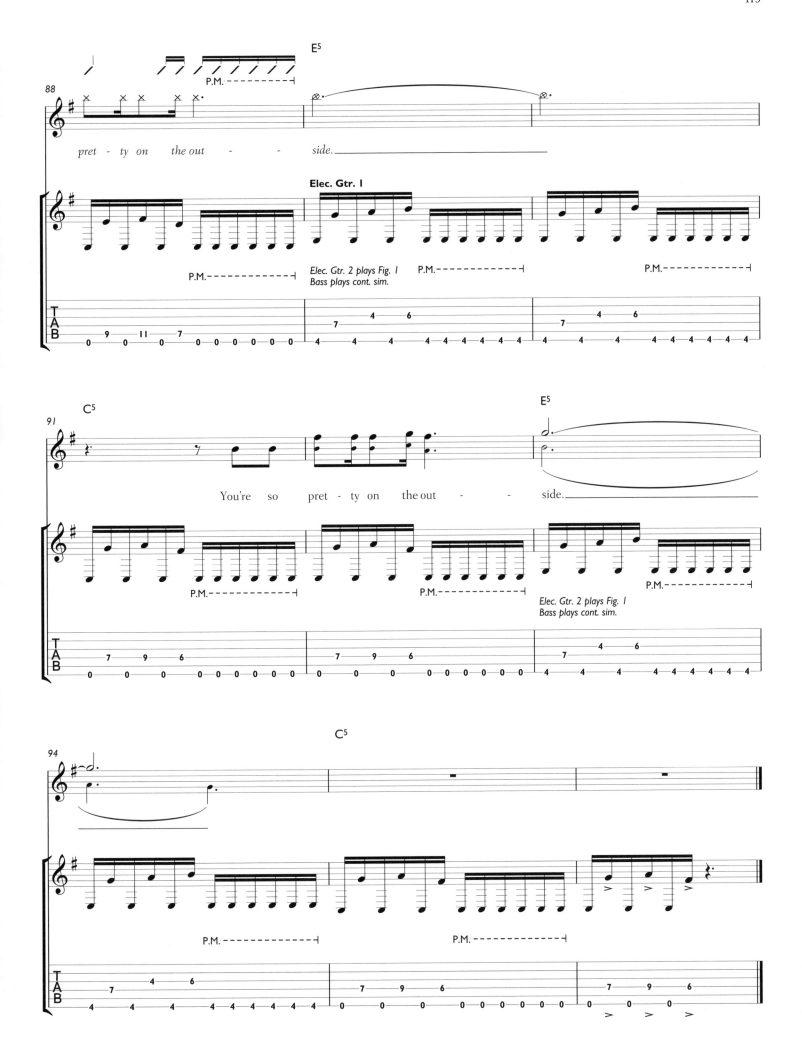